A World of Butterflies
to Color

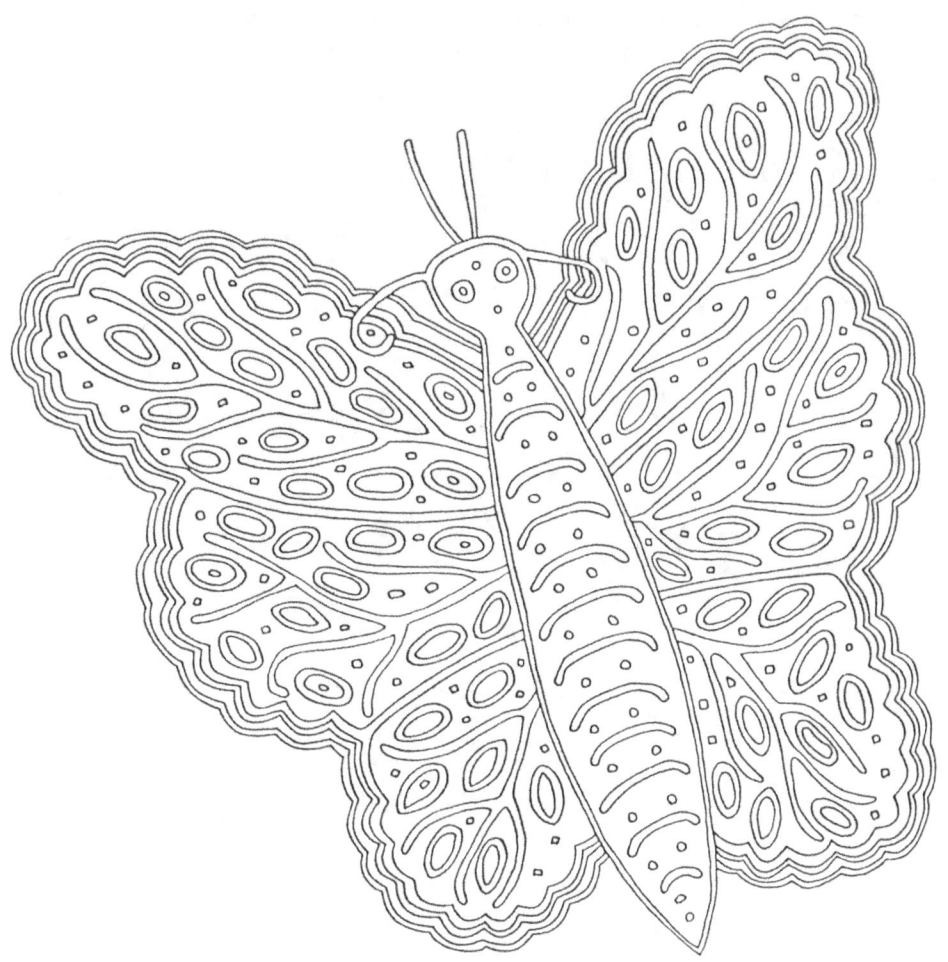

Willow Bascom

ISBN 9798715716071
Independently published
Plymouth, Vermont

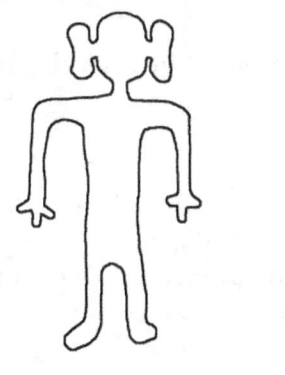

Hi, my name is Willow.

I grew up in Saudi Arabia and Panama, and traveled extensively in Latin America, Europe, Africa, and the Far East. That childhood gave me direct access to the world, and immersed me in the many diverse ways people use color and design to express their perceptions of the world and themselves.

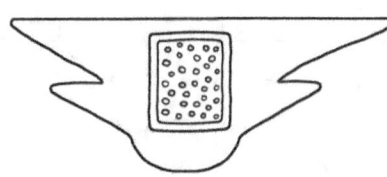

What I find most fascinating is the way so many traditional art styles and design motifs have traveled around the world, carried by cross-cultural migrants to new locales, only to influence and be influenced by the traditions and styles in those new places. Art, I have come to see, is a universal conversation – a visual conversation.

I call this sharing of design styles, motifs and elements World Art. World Art is like World Music, but for your eyes. My art is my contribution to the discussion.

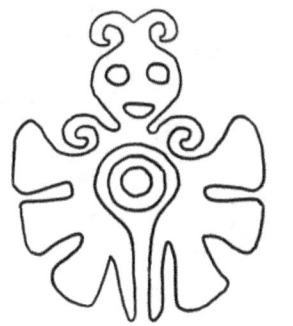

But there is another aspect to my work. I regard it as a gift that came to me from being very ill. For a dozen years I had very active lupus with a lot of cerebral involvement, including a mild stroke. Recovery was a process. First to return was my love of music, then my vocabulary. Prior to my illness I could copy well, but not create art. As I started getting better and realized I couldn't work outside the home I started drawing. My first big project was a multi-cultural ABC book, *Paisley Pig and Friends*. In the process of drawing/writing it, my brain came alive again.

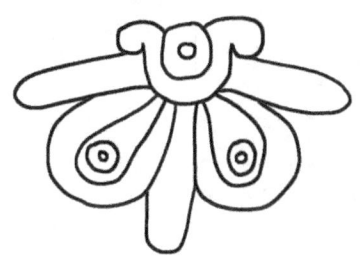

I love drawing and it helped me get my life back. The connections between art and emotion, art and disability, access to our creative selves, and the peace that art (observed or created) gives us, fascinates me. You will notice this influence in many of my butterflies.

I hope you will enjoy coloring these butterflies as much as I enjoyed drawing them. And remember, indigenous art is not constrained by western notions of symmetry, straight lines and the color wheel. When coloring images inspired by traditional cultures, you shouldn't be either!

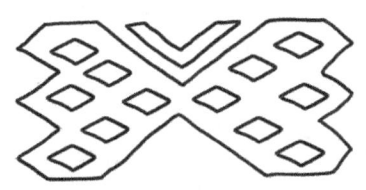

Precolombian Butterfly Representations
From the top:

Zuni Petroglyph of woman with butterfly hairstyle
(I see Princess Leia!), American Southwest

Hopi Pottery butterfly symbol, American Southwest

Aztec Stamp, Central America

Mayan Glyph (writing), Central America

Andean Backstap Weaving, Peru

Gold Butterfly Huaca, Panama

Butterflies and transformation are linked in almost all world cultures. The arrival of butterflies can signal a visit from an angel or departed ancestor, bring good fortune and long life, assist us in accepting change, and even bring courage to a warrior.

People use the media available to them, affecting how intricate their depiction can be. Herein are: butterflies, dragonflies and moths woven into fabric or embroidered upon it; carved into stone or wood; painted on walls, bark cloth, tiles, eggs, vehicles, or ceramics, or cast as jewelry in silver or gold and adorned with precious stones, in styles ranging from prehistoric to pop art! Jump around and color the butterfly whose image or story attracts you. My hope is that when you are finished you will have a visceral awareness of the breadth of humanity's ways of seeing and imparting meaning to our world.

Image	Place of Origin	Info Page
1 BUTTERFLIES 2. PSANKA EGG BUTTERFLIES	Worldwide Ukraine	1
3. HUICHOL BUTTERFLIES 4. KIMONO BUTTERFLIES	Central Mexico Japan	2
5. MOON FLASK 6. DONG BUTTERFLIES 7. MINAKARI ENAMELING	England/China China Persia/present day Iran	3
8. PAKISTANI TRUCK ART 9. DELFT TILES	Pakistan The Netherlands	4
10. BUNDI BUTTERFLY 11. HOPI BUTTERFLY MAIDEN 12. BWA BUTTERFLY MASK	Papua New Guinea USA Southwest West Africa	5
13. MESOAMERICAN STONE BUTTERFLIES 14. HAIDA WOOD CARVING 15. TIBETAN SILVER AMULETS	Pre-Colombian Central America NW Coast USA & Western Canada Tibet	6
16. SPANISH CERAMICS 17. MEXICAN TALAVERA BUTTERFLIES 18. MOLA BUTTERFLY	Spain Mexico Panama - San Blas Islands	7
19. MADHUBANI BUTTERFLY 20. MOTHS 21. ART DECO MOTH	India Worldwide Western Art Movement	8
22. DRAGONFLIES 23. ART NOUVEAU DRAGONFLY 24. CIRCLE OF LIFE	Worldwide Western Art Movement Worldwide	9
Origami Friendship Butterfly	Japan	end of book

Introduction

The people of the Tohono O'odham Nation, located in Arizona, USA and Sonora, Mexico have a wonderful legend about the origin of butterflies. The Creator became sad contemplating the seasonal loss of color of Winter and decreased vitality of humans as they age.

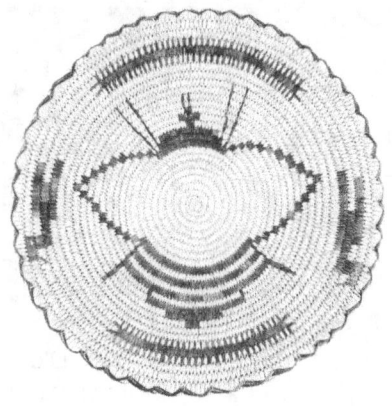

Tohono O'odham Butterfly Basket
Vintage Hand Woven Basket
bradfordsauction.com

> The Creator took out his bag and started gathering things: a spot of sunlight, a handful of blue from the sky, the whiteness of the cornmeal, the shadow of playing children, the blackness of a beautiful girl's hair, the yellow of the falling leaves, the green of the pine needles, the red, purple, and orange of the flowers around him. All these he put into his bag.

He gave the bag to playing children who opened it and...

> hundreds and hundreds of colored butterflies flew out, dancing around the children's heads, settling on their hair, fluttering up again to sip from this or that flower. And the children, enchanted, said that they had never seen anything so beautiful.

Centuries later on the other side of the Atlantic, Moses Harris also connected butterflies with color. He was an English entymologist (someone who studies bugs) and an artist. He drew scientific illustrations of insect life cycles that are admired to this day. His close study of butterfly wings and their many colors informed his invention of the color wheel. Moses said that 660 colors could be made by combining the three "primitives," red, blue, and yellow, using the "painterly art." In the digital age you can play with color online at color.adobe.com/create/color-wheel.

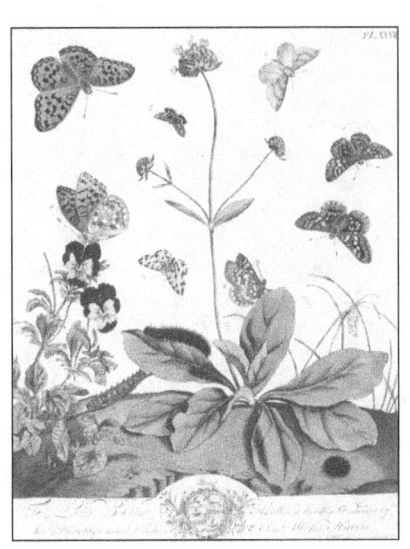

A plate from Moses Harris' book *The Aurelius*

Moses Harris' color wheel (so sorry it is not in color) hand colored for each edition of his book, *The Natural System of Color.*

Coloring Page Descriptions

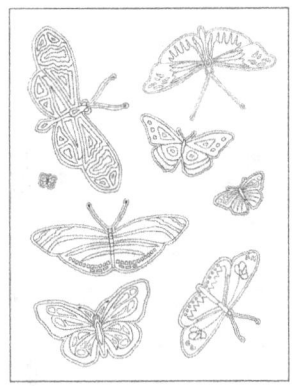

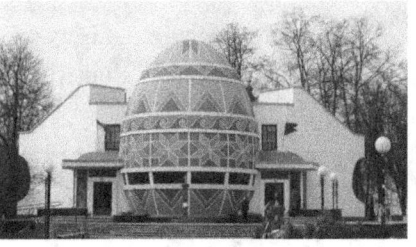

Pysanka Museum
Kolomyia, Ukraine has a collection of over 10,000 eggs
uauk.files.wordpress.com

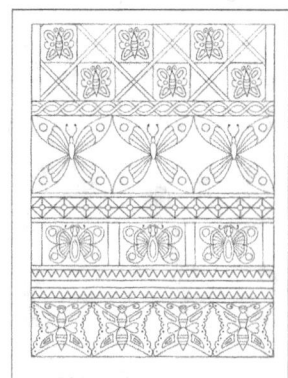

1. BUTTERFLIES Their beauty, variety of patterns, sizes, and colors are awe inspiring! They are also pretty tough. Some butterflies migrate many hundreds of miles. Add cultural depictions and symbolism from around the globe and the lovely butterfly will take *you* on quite a journey!

2. PYSANKA EGG BUTTERFLIES In the Ukraine making Psanky eggs is an Easter tradition. Pysanky eggs are decorated with a wax-resist method similar to the making of batik fabric in Indonesia. In eastern Europe butterflies symbolize angels.

"As long as people paint pysanky, there will be love in the world."

old Ukranian saying

1

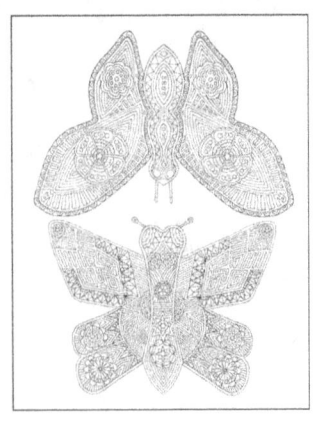

3. HUICHOL BUTTERFLIES

The Huichol People live in central Mexico. One of their best-known creations is the yarn "eye of god" which many of us have made. They also make intricate colorful pictures to represent dreams and visions. The butterflies recreated here are inspired by huichol bead art. For many Mesoamerican peoples their culture, stored in flower's seeds, is spread by butterflies. And like societies worldwide butterflies are considered a symbol of transformation and good fortune.

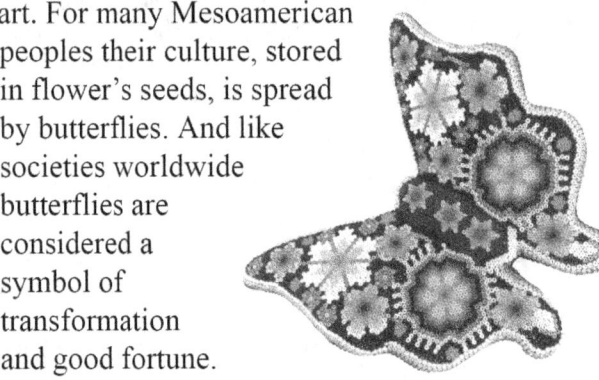

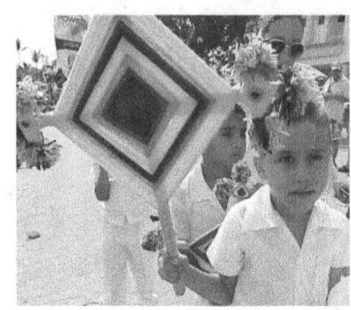

parade for
"Ojos de Dios"
with children
of many ages.
Sol Mexico News

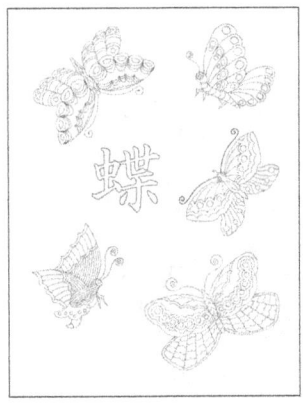

4. KIMONO BUTTERFLIES

Japanese art abounds with butterflies and symbolize many things. When someone dies it is thought their soul transforms into a butterfly on its journey to eternal life. They can also represent the unfolding of a girl into womanhood.

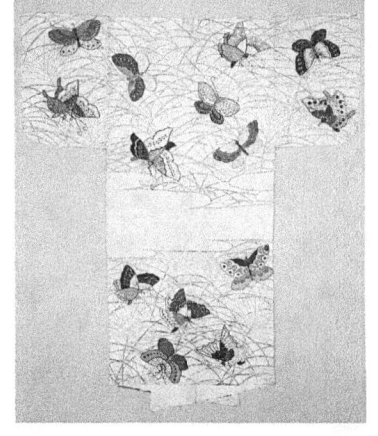

Noh robe
17th century Japan
Metropolitan Museum of Art
New York City

Japanese family crests, *mon*, originated as fabric designs woven into the formal robes worn at the Imperial court. Over time these designs became emblems used as identifiers by high-ranking families and then warriors. The *mons* below show the variety in Japanese butterfly designs.

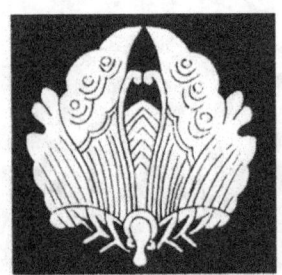  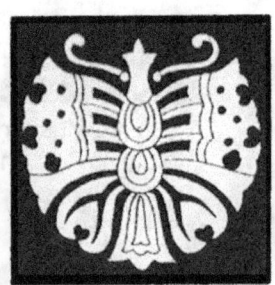 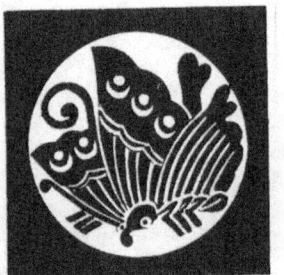 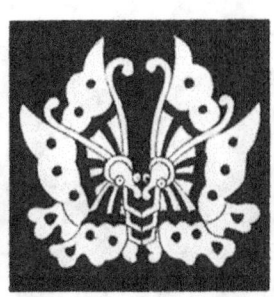

From *Japanese Design Motifs: 4,260 Illustrations of Heraldic Crests*
Dover Publications, 1972.

"Once upon a time, I, Chuang Chou, dreamt I was a butterfly, fluttering hither and thither, to all intents and purposes a butterfly. I was conscious only of my happiness as a butterfly, unaware that I was Chou. Soon I awaked, and there I was, veritably myself again. Now I do not know whether I was then a man dreaming I was a butterfly, or whether I am now a butterfly, dreaming I am a man."

2   venerated Chinese philosopher also known as Zhuangzi

5. MOON FLASK

Originally created in 15th century China, a "moon-embracing-flask" has flat sides and is shaped like the full moon.

After Japan opened to the West in the mid-1800s many European porcelain manufacturers inspired by Asian arts melded Western and Eastern sensibilities.

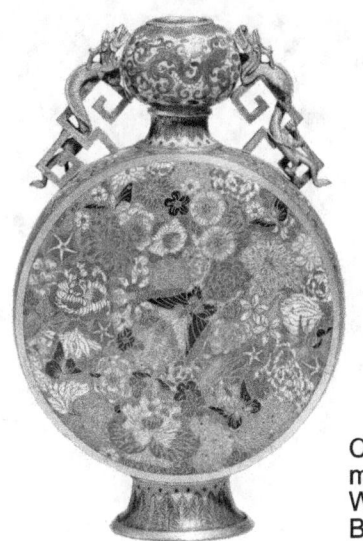

Chinese cloisonné enamel
moon flask vase c.1800
Walters Art Museum
Baltimore, MD

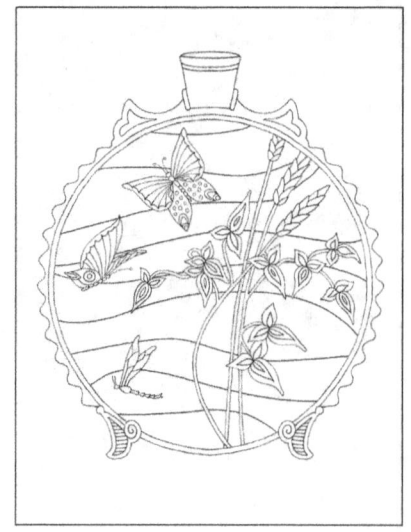

6. DONG BUTTERFLIES

For the Dong Tribe of China the butterfly is a symbol of long life, joy, and warmth. They embroider and appliqué intricate beautiful designs for baby carriers and clothing.

I imagine a loving mother-to-be wishing to bestow the attributes of butterflies upon her baby by embroidering butterflies on a baby carrier.

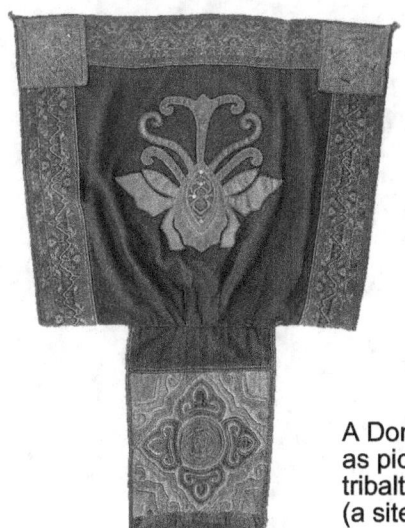

A Dong baby carrier
as pictured on
tribaltrappings.com
(a site worth exploring!)

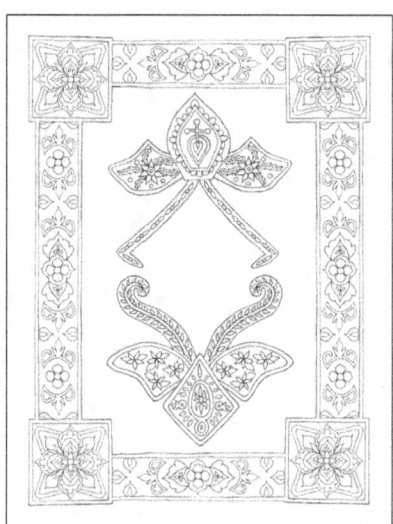

7. MINAKARI ENAMELING

is the art of intricately decorating metals and ceramics with a glaze that is then fired at very high heat. Mina means heaven in Persian and is represented by the blue color. This art form has been practiced for at least three thousand years. Everything from jewelry to mosques are gloriously ornamented with a touch of heaven.

Butterflies symbolize faithful love in Eastern thought, a deep willingness to sacrifice oneself for love.

There is a long tradition of using the flowing lines of Arabic calligraphy to form shapes out of words. Here a poem by Persian Sufi master Rumi is written/drawn as a butterfly.

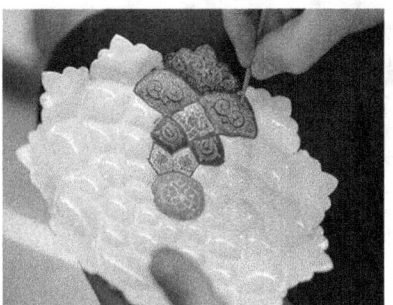

Minakari platter in process
Photo by beytoote.com
hamkarbashi.com

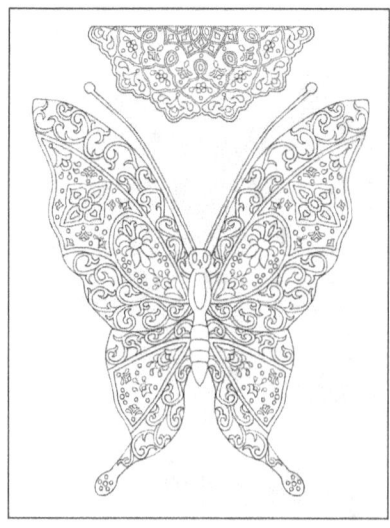

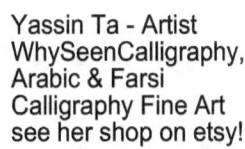

Yassin Ta - Artist
WhySeenCalligraphy,
Arabic & Farsi
Calligraphy Fine Art
see her shop on etsy!

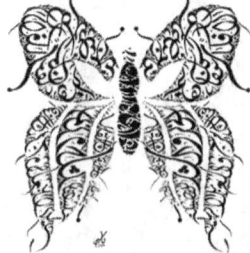

Out beyond ideologies of right and wrong doing,
There lies an endless field, I'll meet you there.
-Rumi

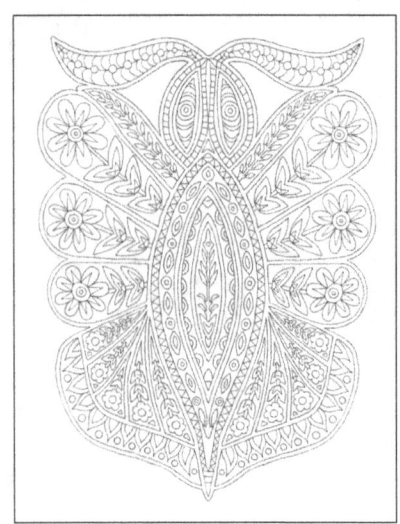

8. PAKISTANI TRUCK ART

Growing up in Panama I loved the colorful chivas, buses used throughout Latin America. Pakistan is also known for intricately painting and decorating their trucks, buses and taxis. When in Saudi Arabia I saw donkey and camel carts that were works of art!

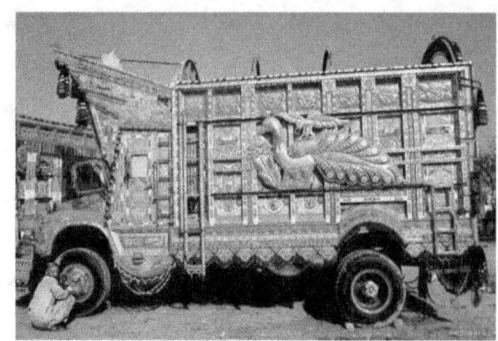

Haider Ali
professional truck artist
Check out his facebook
page to see more art.

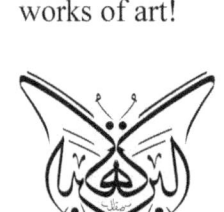

The Arabic word for butterfly, al-Baraka, forms a butterfly. Arabic zoomorphic calligraphy Mamoun Sakkal 2003 sakkal.com

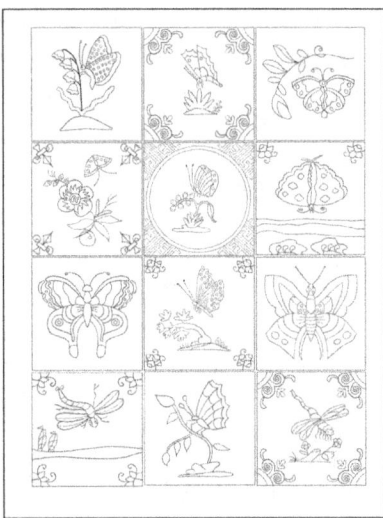

9. DELFT TILES

Delft is a town in the Netherlands renowned for its blue and white pottery. From palaces to farmhouses, whole walls have traditionally been decorated with tiles.

While most countries have one national animal, the Netherlands has three: squirrel, swan, and butterfly.

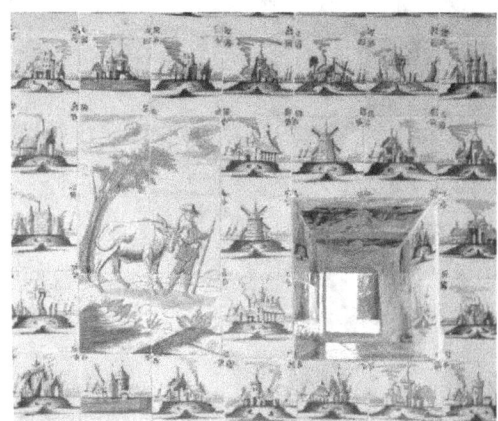

Farmhouse wall
covered with
Delft tiles
wikipedia

So many tiles, so many styles, and yet... all butterflies!

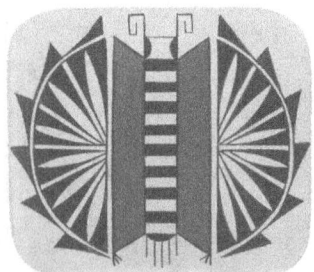

North American SW - Hopi
Garrett Maho
Museum of Northern Arizona

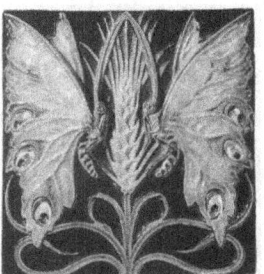

Portugal - Art Nouveau
Rafael Bordallo Pinhiero
British Museum

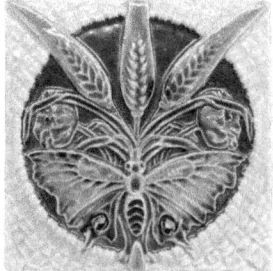

Portugal - embossed
Bordallo Pinheiro

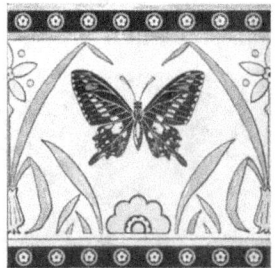

England - Gothic
Christopher Dresser

Michigan USA
Arts and Crafts Revival

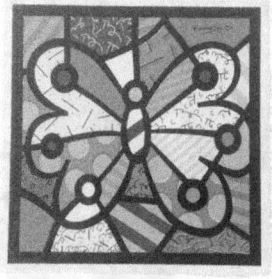

Brazil - Neo-Pop
Romero Britto

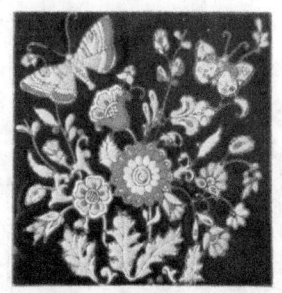

Greece - Folk Art
Smaltotechniki Ceramics

Mexico
Vintage Talavera

10. <u>BUNDI BUTTERFLY DANCE</u> In Papua New Guinea barkcloth is used to make butterfly wings. Men constuct the wings in the forest and then women perform the dance.

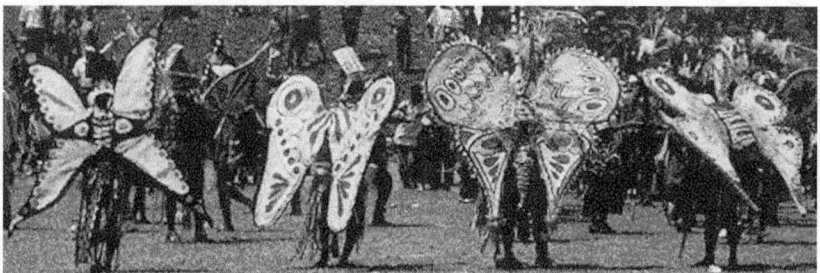

art-pacific.com
images and cultural info

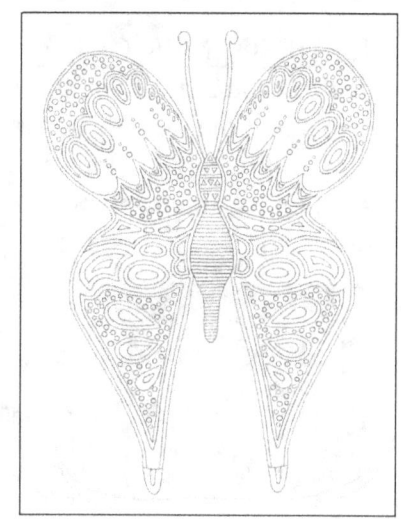

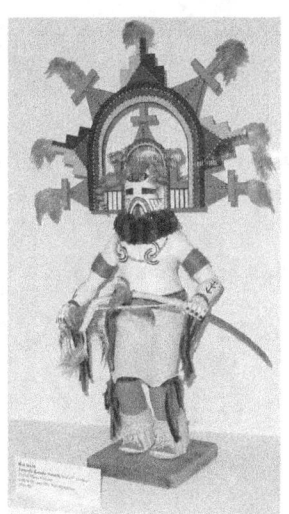

11. <u>HOPI BUTTERFLY MAIDEN</u> These are Kachina or Katsina dolls made by the Hopi for their butterfly dance. It takes place in gratitude for the corn harvest, with prayers for rain and blessings. Hopi girls and their partners must learn thirty-two dances for the two day ceremony.

Danforth Museum
Framingham, MA USA

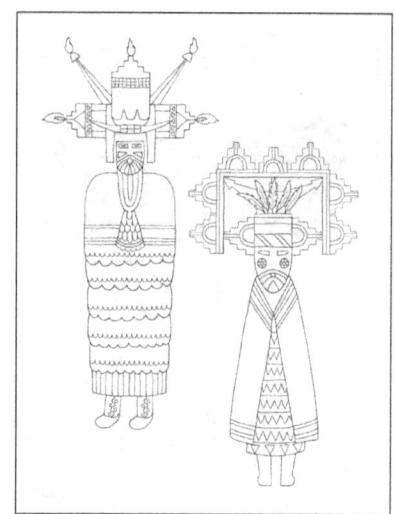

12. <u>BWA BUTTERFLY MASK</u> In the Spring the Bwa people of West Africa hold a butterfly dance to celebrate new growth and fertility. Men wear the heavy wooden butterfly-shaped masks to beseech ancestors to bestow good fortune upon them.

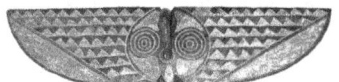

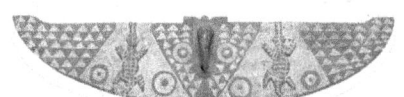

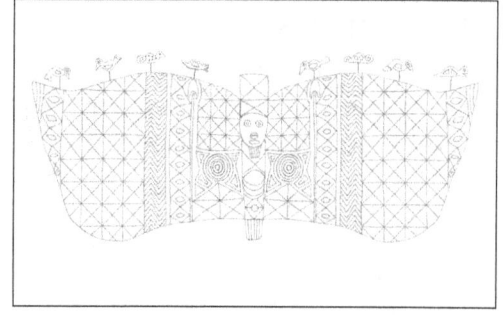

found on AuthenticAfrica.com

found on Pagodared.com

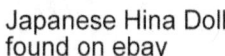

In Japan a Girl's Day Festival is held on the third day of the third month. To protect daughters from evil spirits Hina dolls are displayed. This Butterfly Dancer Hina doll is welcoming the opening of peach blossoms in the Spring.

In Bulgaria there is a butterfly ritual held to bring rain. A young girl is festooned with greenery and waves leafy branches as if they were butterfly wings. She and other young girls visit homes, wells, and springs to prevent drought.

Japanese Hina Doll
found on ebay

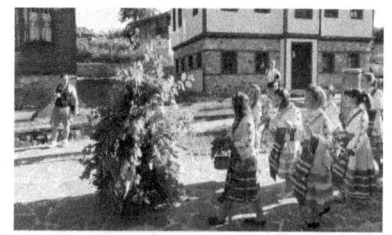

Peperuda ritual, Bulgaria
heritages.info

13. MESOAMERICAN STONE BUTTERFLIES Civilizations rose and fell and butterfly associations changed too. They are thought to be the soul of the recently departed and suggest immortality and reincarnation. But butterflies are also a poweful symbol used by warriors, representing fire and death. The designs pictured here are from clay stamps used to decorate pots, fabric, paper, or at festival times, the body.

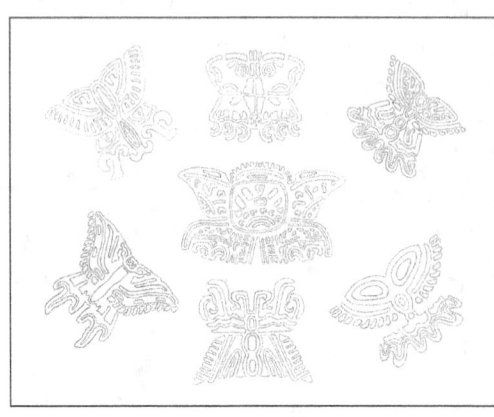

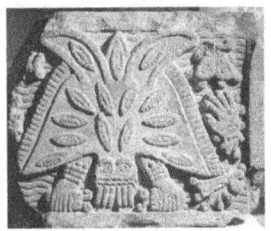

Stone altar of Itzpapalotl
Mesoamerican Warrior Goddess
National Museum of Anthropology
Mexico City.

14. HAIDA WOOD CARVING The Haida people believe the butterfly represents grace and balance in their acceptance of change. The butterfly is thought of as a messenger to the Haida as well as a scout and spokesperson for the Raven.

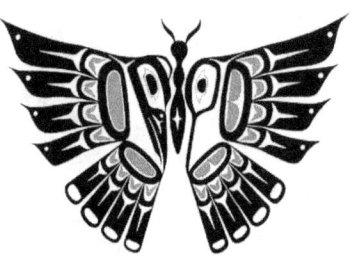

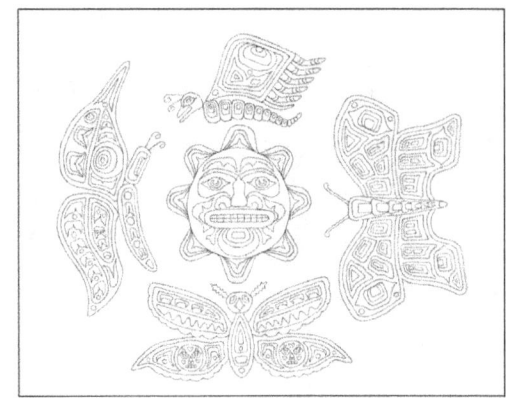

artwork by Lon French
Haida Raven Art
note the butterfly wings are
a raven and a hummingbird!

15. TIBETAN SILVER AMULETS Amulets are tools; something physical upon which to focus thoughts and prayers. These Tibetan butterflies are meant to remind you not to hold on to your sorrow and problems, and thus transform your life like the butterfly does.

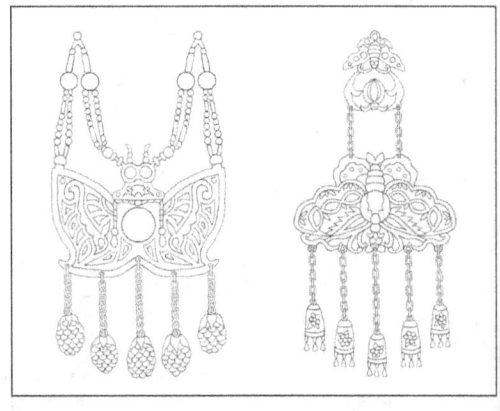

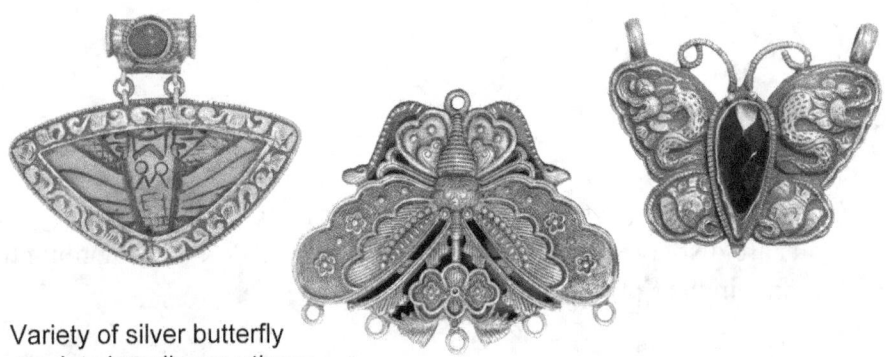

Variety of silver butterfly
amulets in online auctions

*What the caterpillar perceives as the end,
to the butterfly is just the beginning.*

Buddhist saying

16. SPANISH CERAMICS

To keep glazes from running the *cuerda seca* technique is used. A fine cord outlines each shape and adds dimension to the finished ceramic. In Christianity, Spain's predominant religion, the butterfly symbolizes three steps in faith. The hungry caterpillar represents peoples' earthly focus on physical needs. The cocoon symbolizes the tomb, and the butterfly is the resurrection free of material cares.

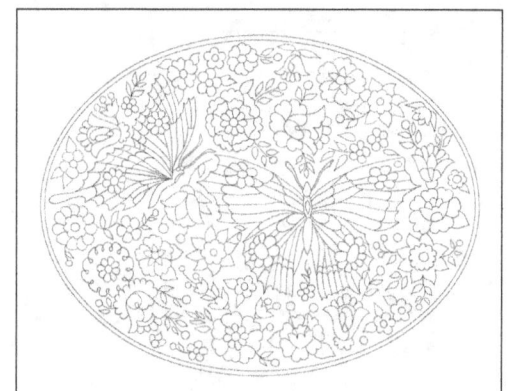

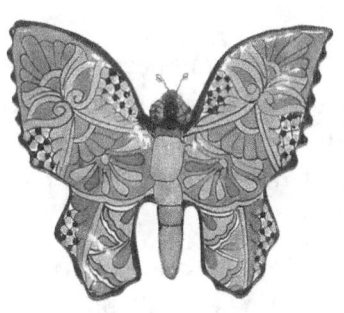

A new handmade plate carrying on the cuerda seca tradition.

17. MEXICAN TALAVERA BUTTERFLIES

Artisans from Talavera, Spain introduced their style of creating ceramics to Mexico in the Colonial period. Mexican artisan/artists have used it as a springboard to create a style unique to their culture. Monarch butterflies migrate from North America to the Sierra Madre Mountains in Mexico, arriving on November first - the Day of the Dead - where they are thought to be the spirits of loved ones returning.

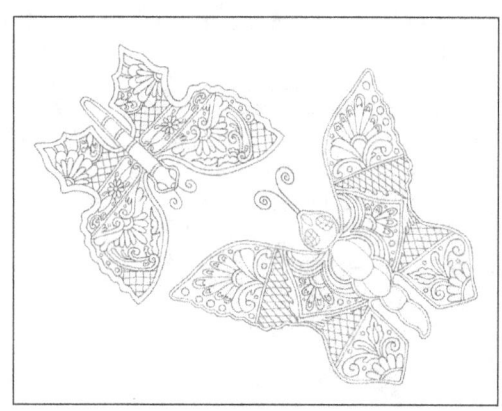

Talavera Butterfly

18. MOLA BUTTERFLY

While living in Panama I collected molas, the cloth panels sewn and worn by Guna women. The Guna live very close to nature and molas are filled with birds, animals, and plants from the rainforest around them. All things are believed to have a spirit, *Purba*, connected to them.

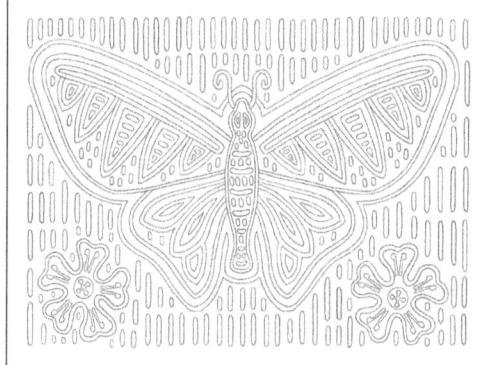

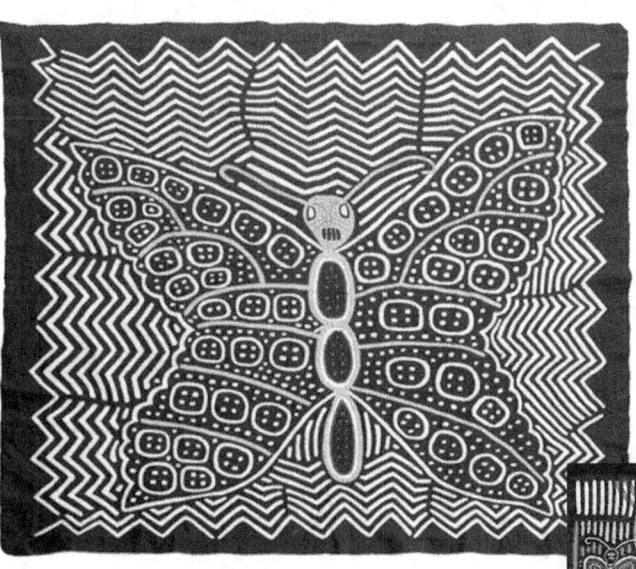

large mola, made to order

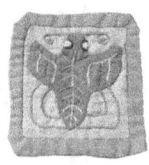

mola patch - encouraged by the Peace Corp in the 60s.

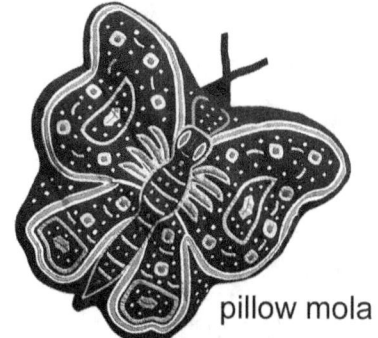

pillow mola

traditional mola for blouse

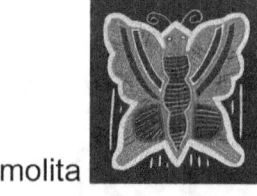

molita

7

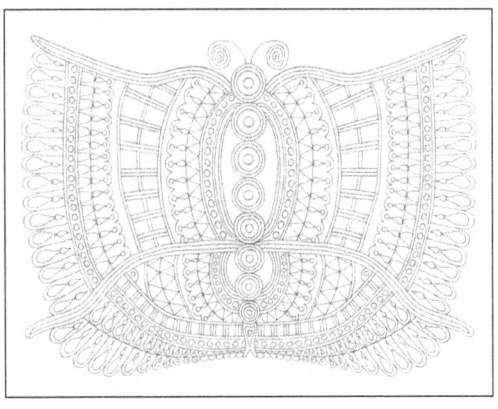

19. <u>MADHUBANI BUTTERFLY</u> This art style originated in the Madhubani region of India as wall art to celebrate gods, life events or festivals. In Hinduism, practiced in much of India, butterflies have a dual meaning. The belief in reincarnation and the value of meditation to transform ourselves is represented in the butterflys' emergence from the cocoon.

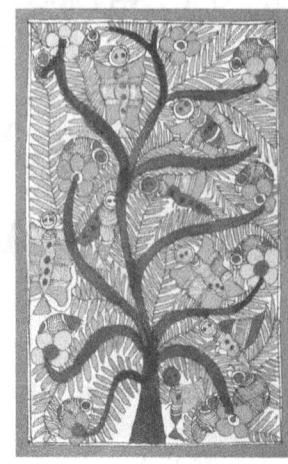

exoticindiaart.com is the souce of the two styles of Mdhubani butterflies used here.

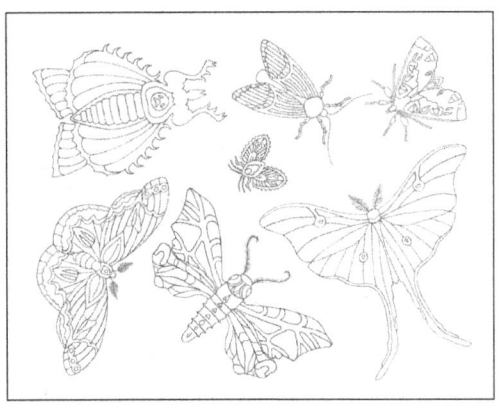

20. <u>MOTHS</u> Most moths are shades of brown and gray because they are active at night. There are exceptions, nocturnal butterflies and moths flitting about by day, but the one sure difference is the feathery antennae of moths. As bats use sonar to navigate in the dark, moths antennae pick up scents to guide their way.

While there are many more varieties of moths than butterflies there are fewer myths and meanings accorded to them. For Yacqui shamans the moth is the bearer and giver of wisdom. In Appalachian and Celtic folk tales a moth means the presence of an ancestor.

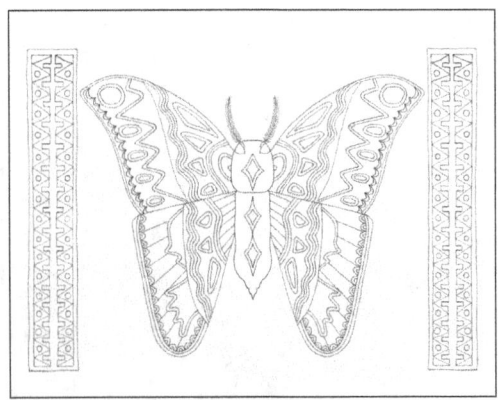

21. <u>ART DECO MOTH</u> Art Deco was a style developed in the mid-1920s known for combining ethnic designs with geometric shapes. To me this moth has a Navajo feel to it. The fusion of Southwestern tribal styles with Art Deco was popular in both art and architecture and became known as Pueblo Deco.

Spanish Moon Moth
Looks like Art Deco!
posted on reddit
by u/Mass1m01973

One of my favorite science fiction authors captures a common perception of moths as he describes a charactor in his novel, Ubik.

He felt all at once like an ineffectual moth, fluttering at the windowpane of reality, dimly seeing it from outside.

Philip K. Dick

22. DRAGONFLIES

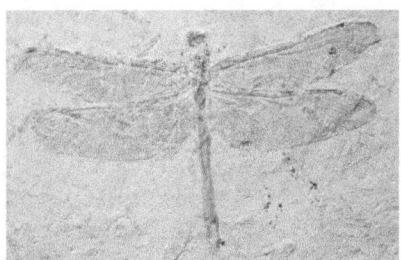

Early Cretaceous fossil
Wingspan of 30 inches/75 cm!
The Virtual Fossil Museum
fossilmuseum.net

Dragonflies appear in the fossil record about 300 million years ago, prior to butterflies. Eggs are laid in water so instead of a cocoon they have a nymph stage.

In Japan dragonflies are revered for strength and agility. In ancient times Japan was called Dragonfly Island.

For the Zuni dragonflies symbolize rain, harvest, and summer.

Dragonfly names and reputations vary widely across cultures. These are just a few: Austria: Eye Sticker
Belgium: Madonna's Horse, Devil
Armenia: Rose-Butterfly
Saudi Arabia: The Fan
USA: Devil's Darning Needle, Snake Bunny
Sweden: Water Maiden, Fairy Spindle

23. ART NOUVEAU DRAGONFLY LADY
Leaving straight lines behind, Art Nouveau (literally New Art in French) was a Western art movement that overlapped with Art Deco. It applied flowing lines from nature and an appreciation of female beauty. Although only popular from 1890-1910 you can see its resurgance in 60s pop art.

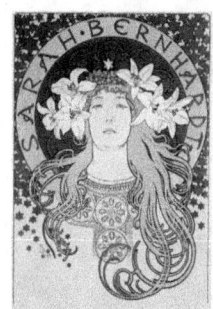

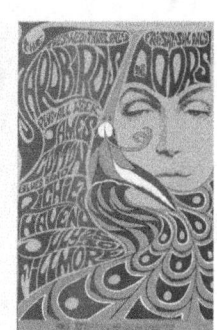

Alfons Mucha
1896

Bonnie Maclean
1967

thanks to retroavangarda.com

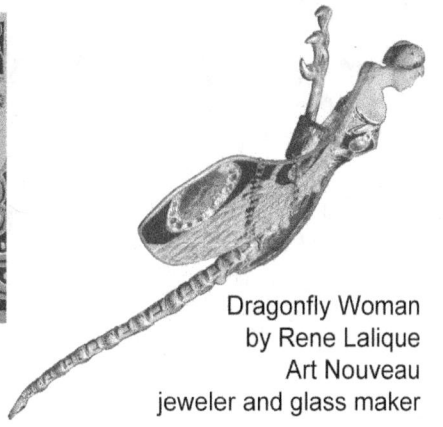

Dragonfly Woman
by Rene Lalique
Art Nouveau
jeweler and glass maker

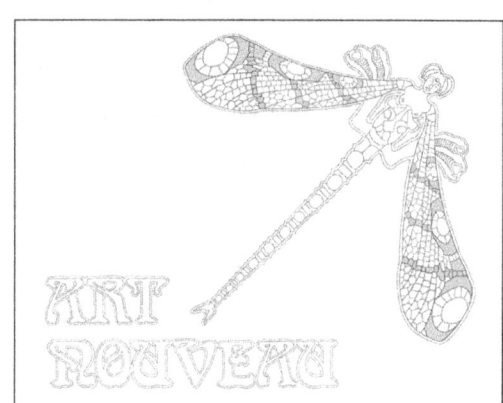

24. CIRCLE OF LIFE
"Nature's way of taking and giving back life to earth. It symbolizes the universe being sacred and divine. It represents the infinite nature of energy, meaning if something dies it gives new life to another." (Collins Dictionary) Butterflies, dragonflies, and moths are vital, serving as pollinators, pest control for farmers, vital nutrition in the food chain, and they even create the strands from which we weave silk and strengthen parachutes and bicycle tires, and have many more indusrial uses.

They also fill our hearts with their beauty and are messengers and symbols we use to understand and share our perceptions of the world.

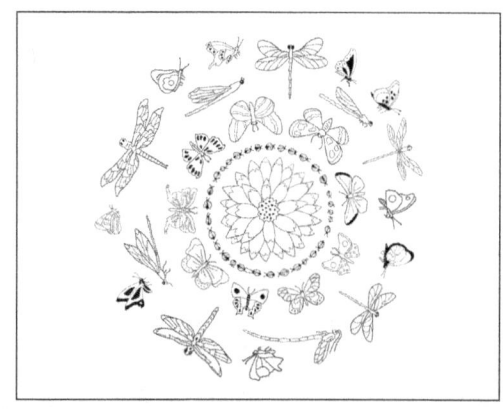

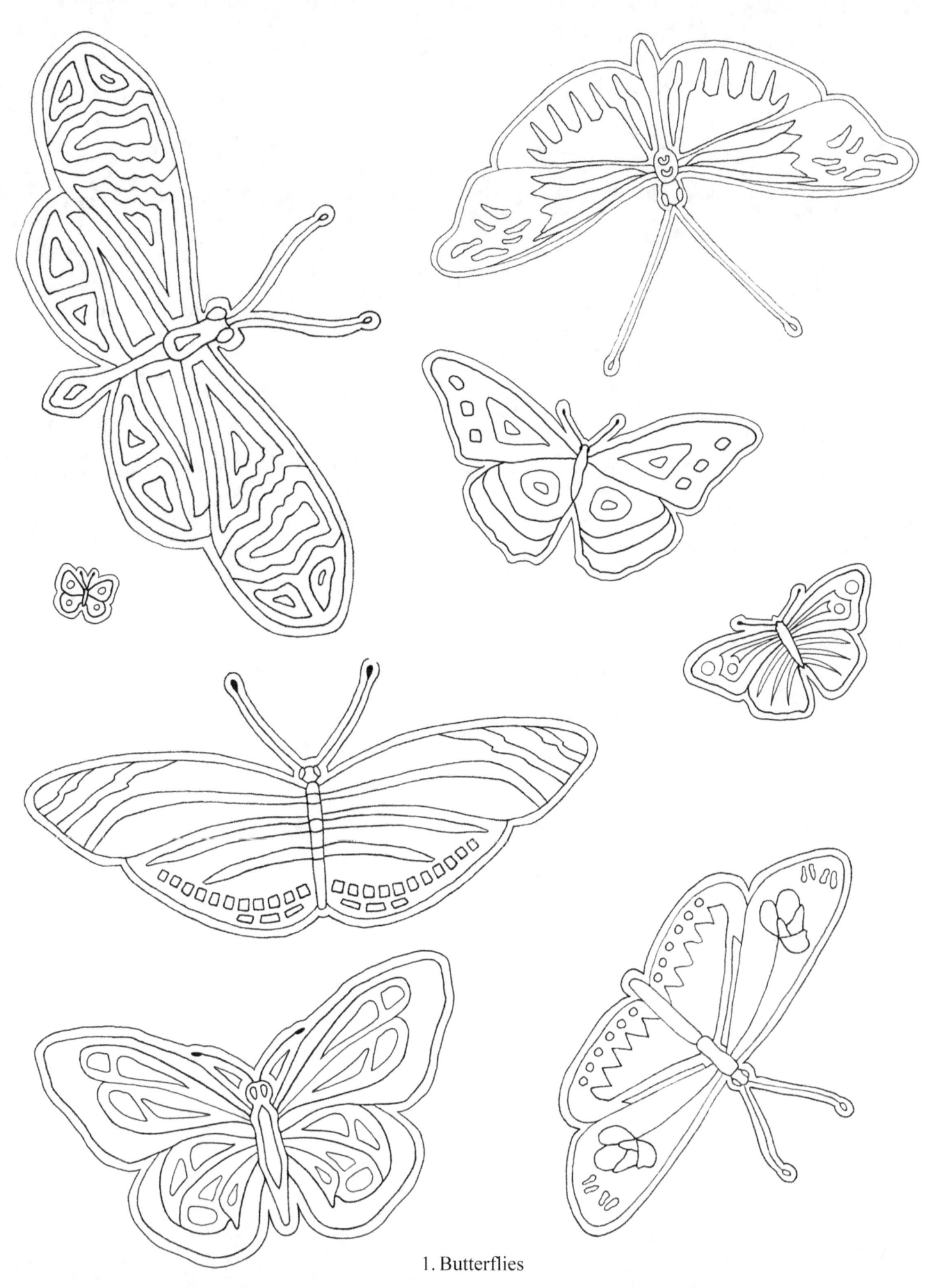

1. Butterflies

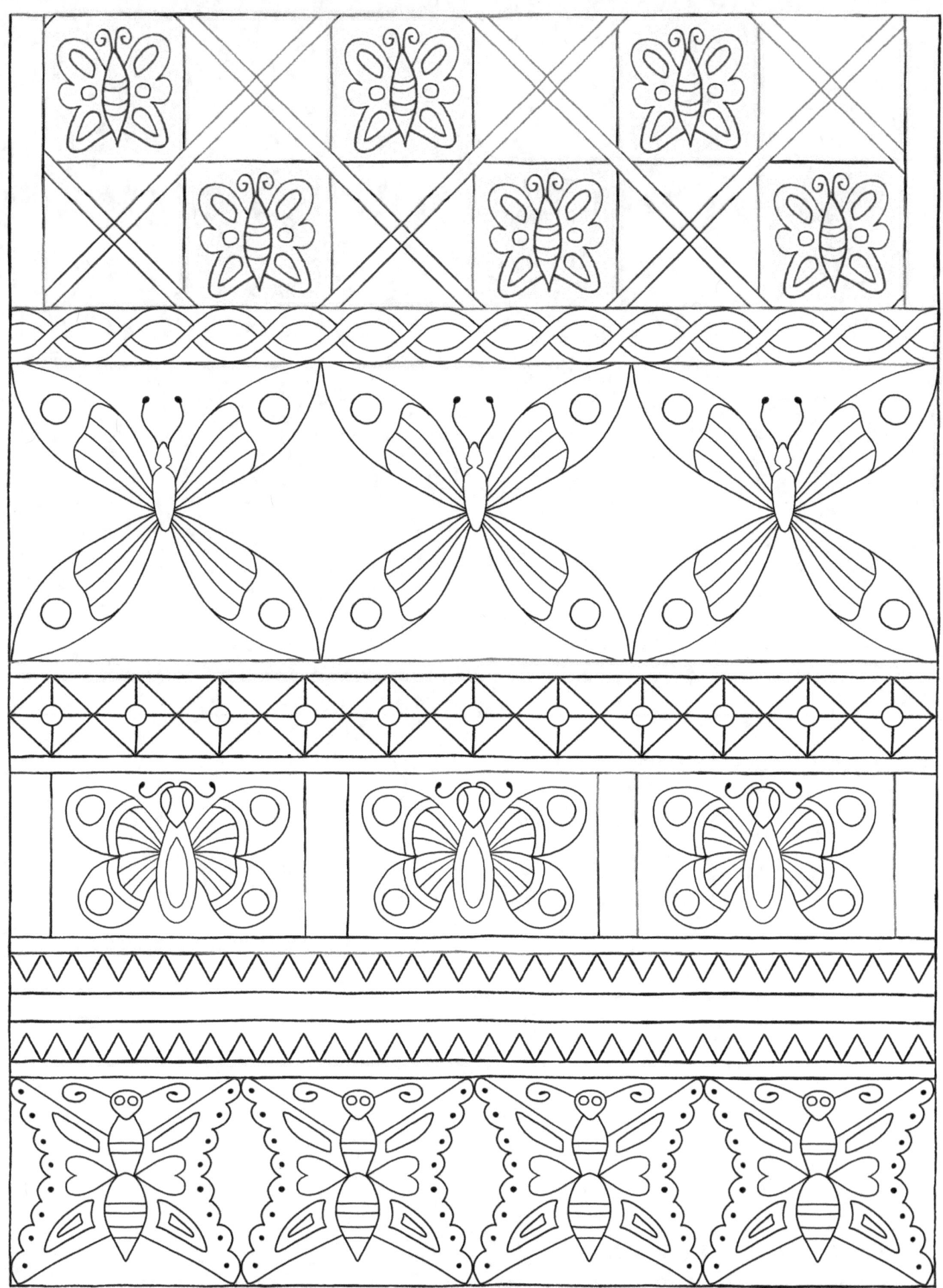

2. Pysanka Egg Butterflies

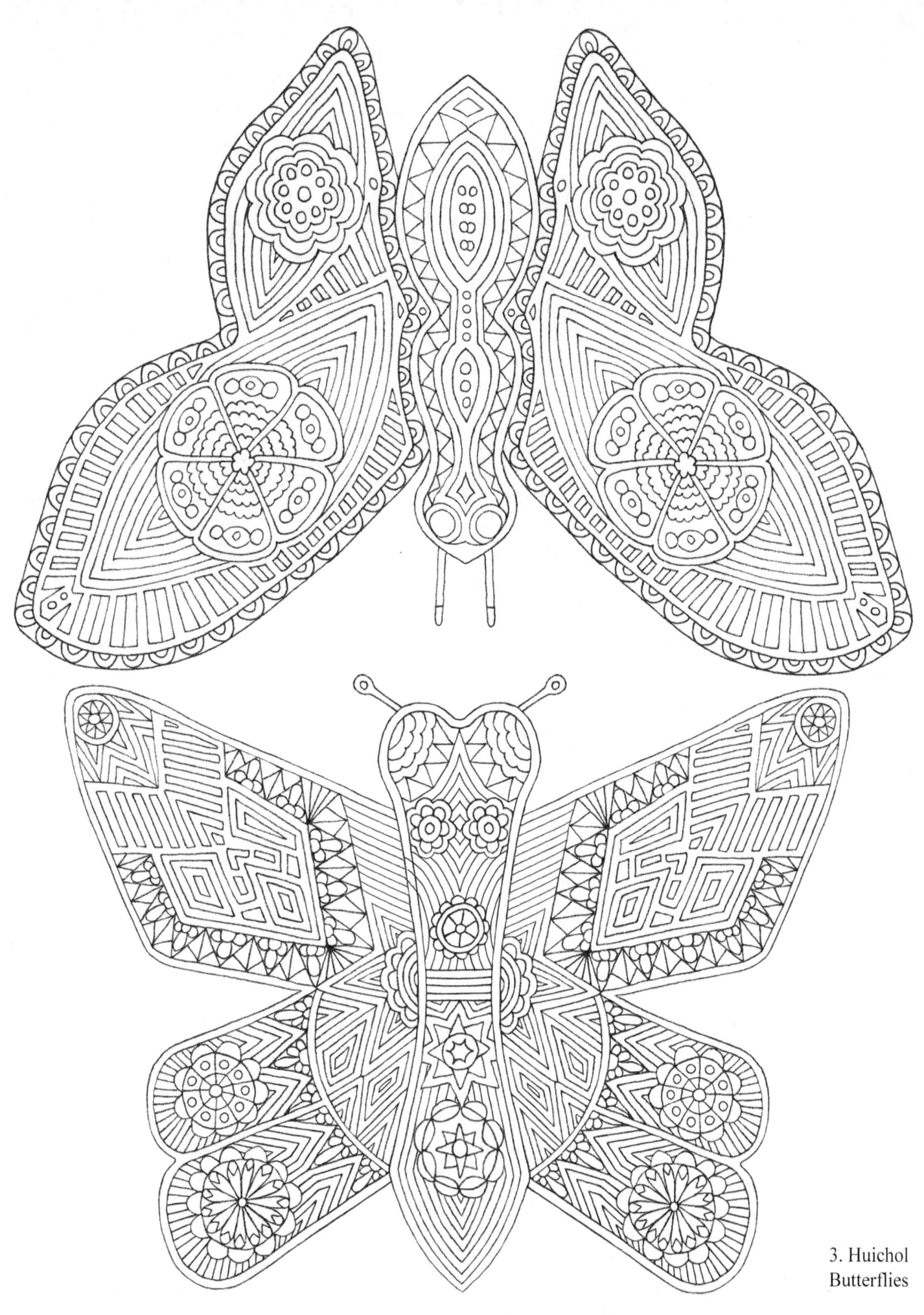

3. Huichol
Butterflies

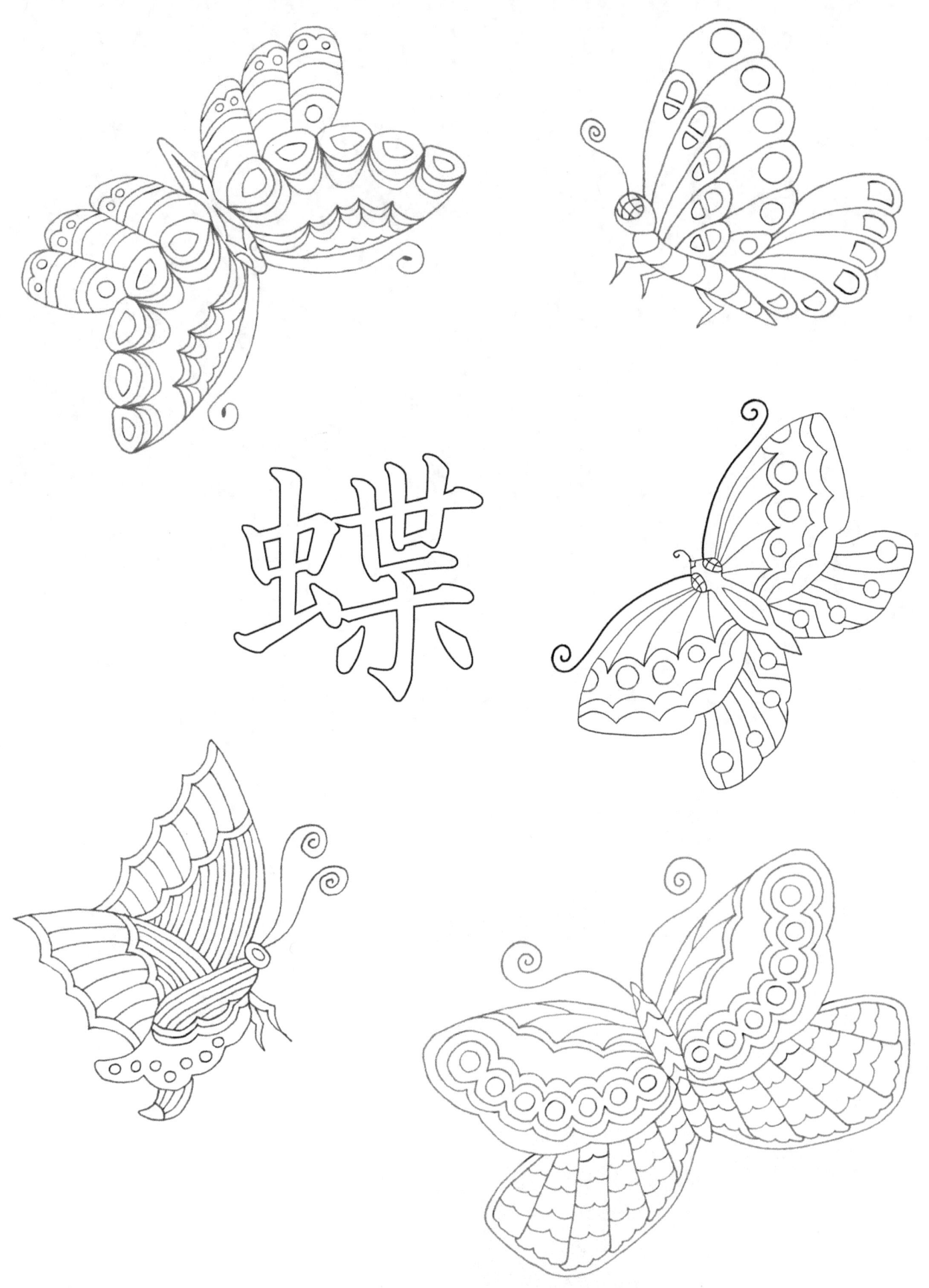

蝶

4. Kimono Butterflies

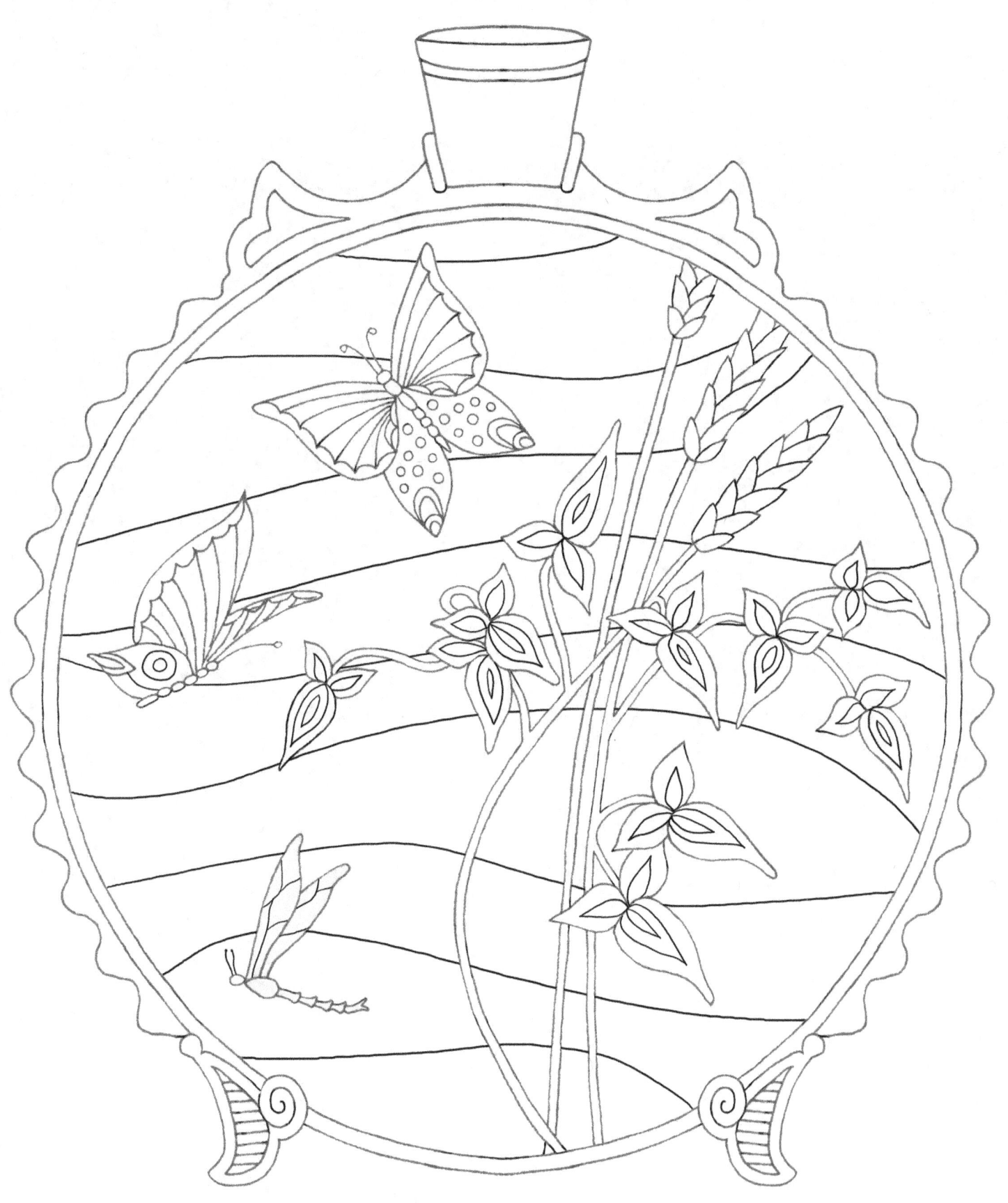

5. Moon Flask

6. Dong Butterflies

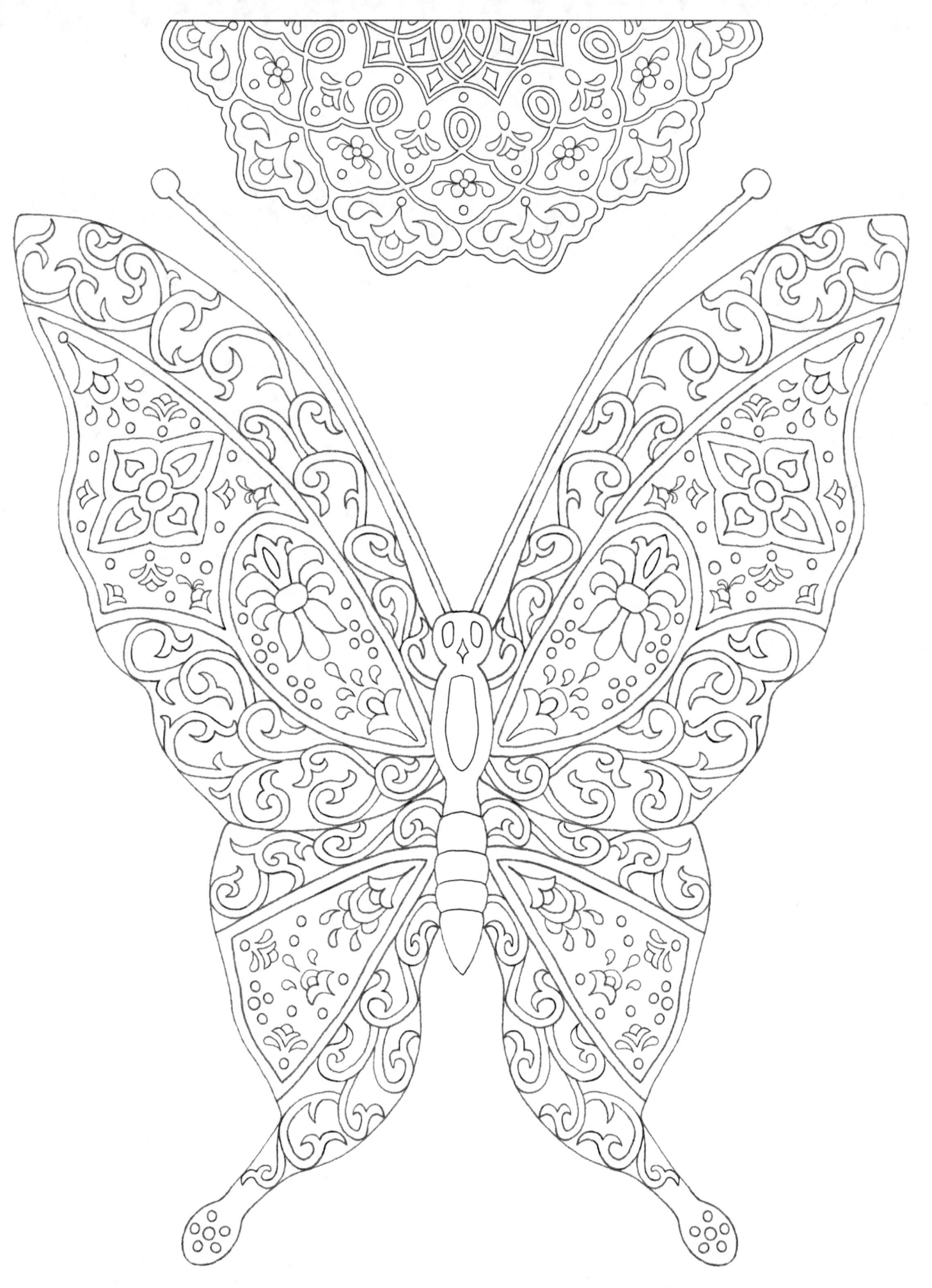

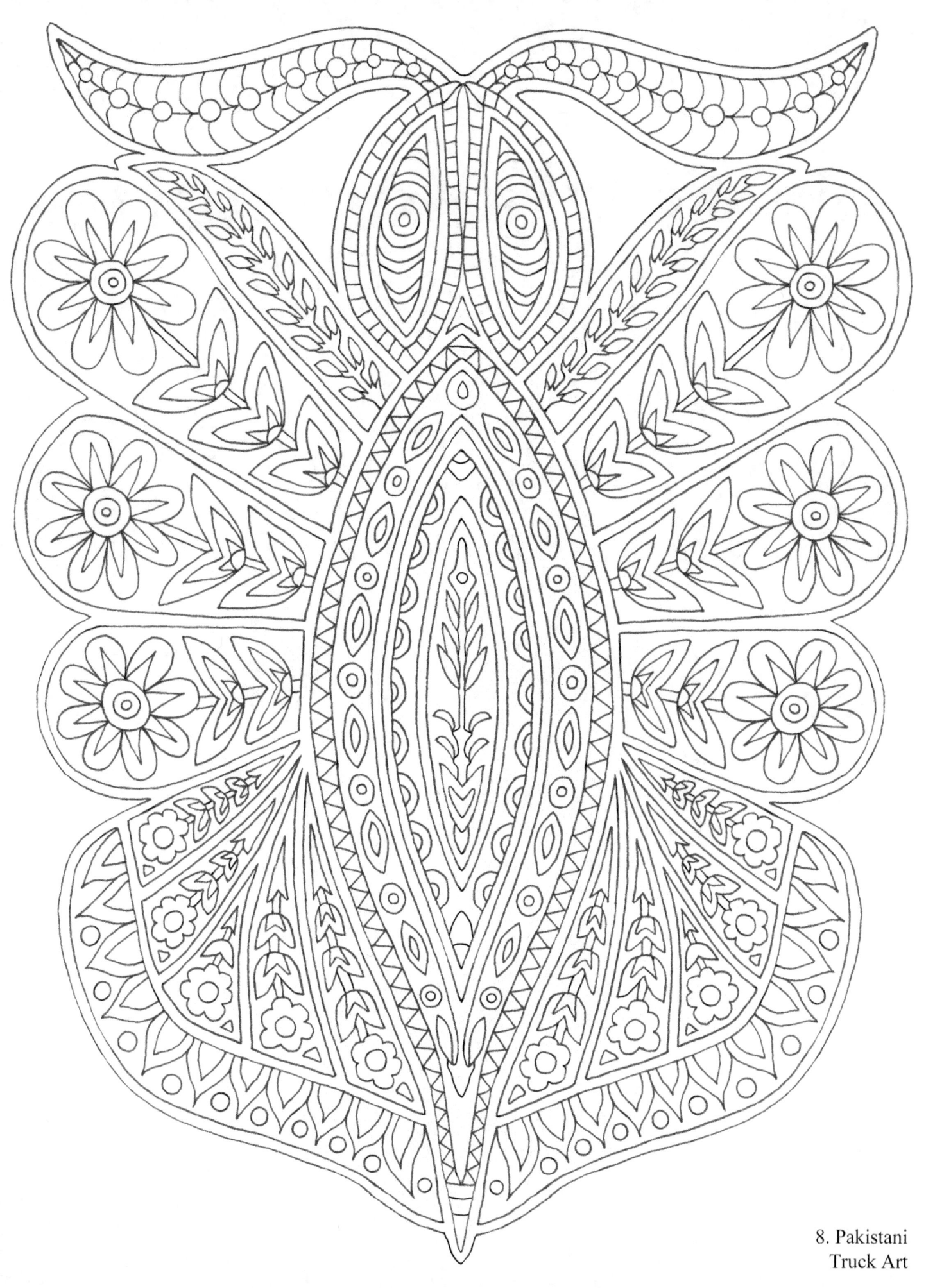

8. Pakistani
Truck Art

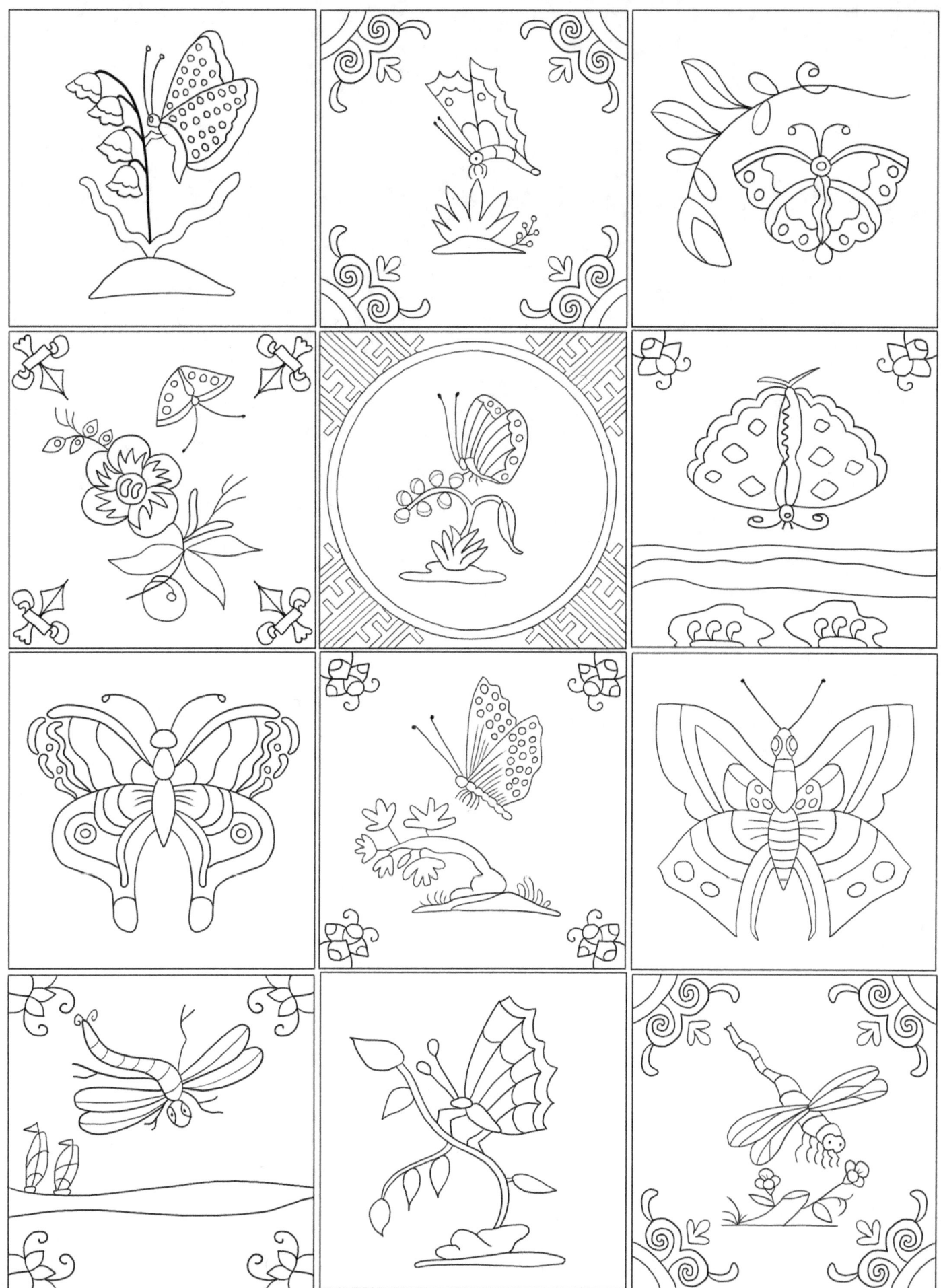

9. Delft Tiles

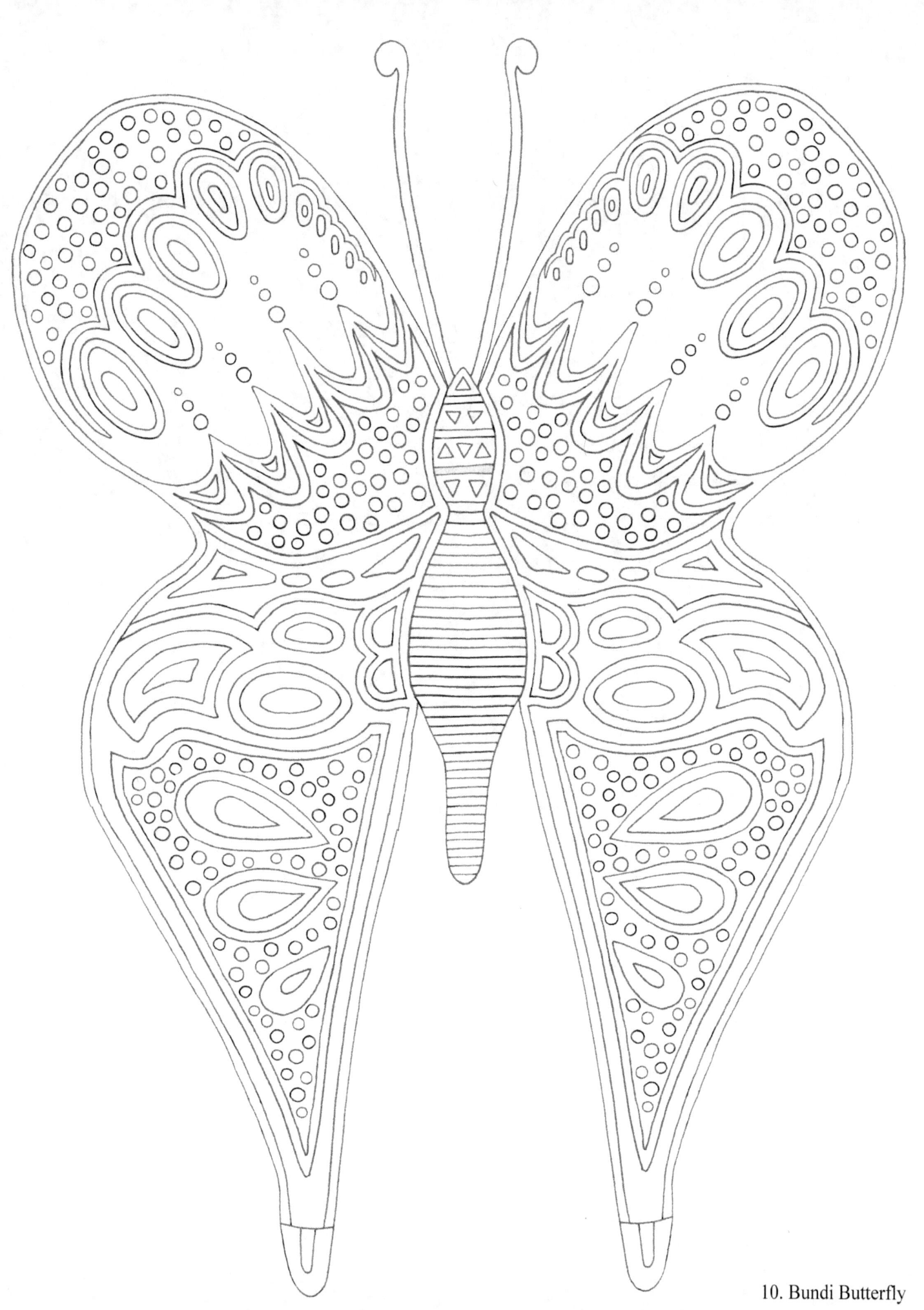

10. Bundi Butterfly

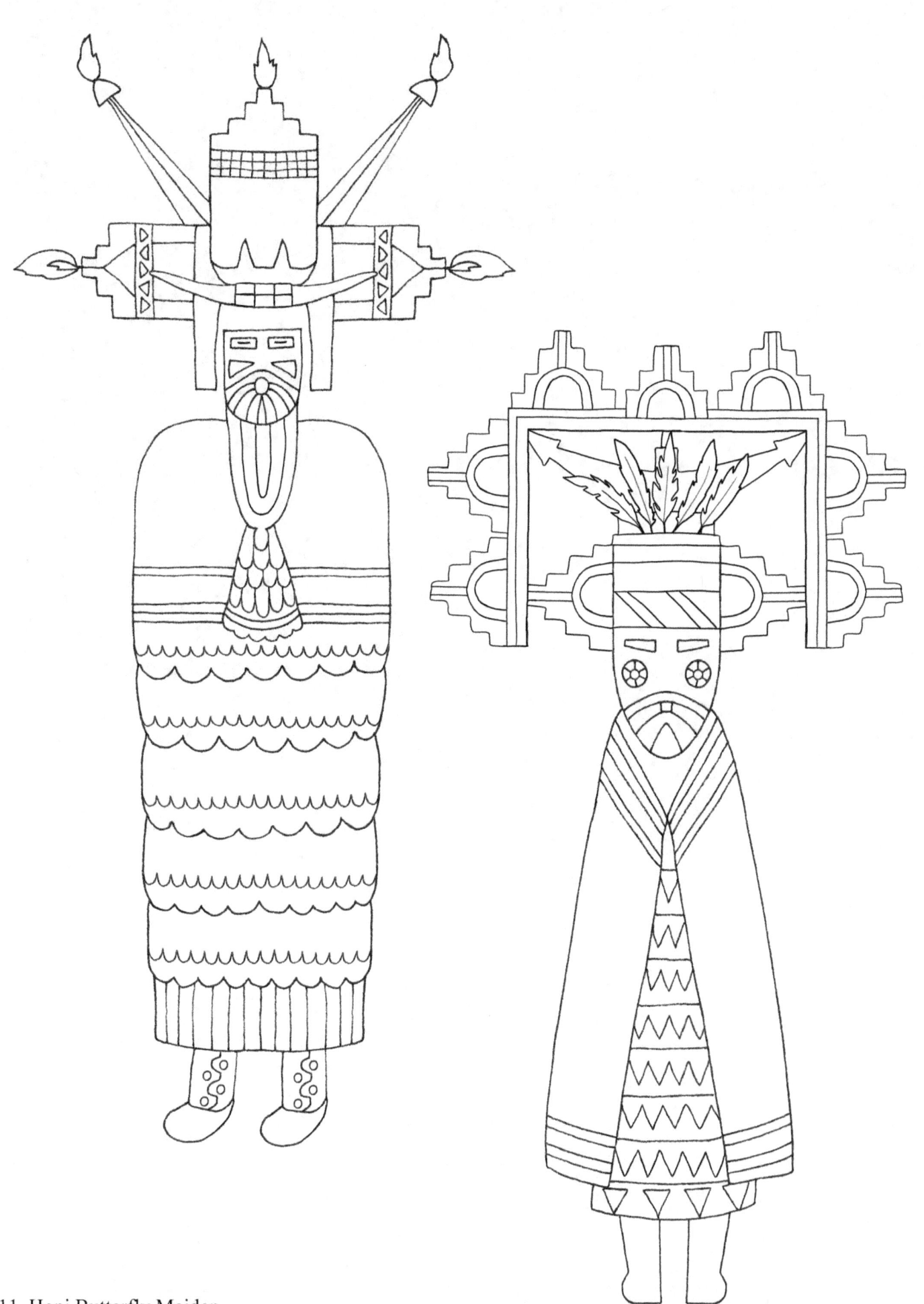

11. Hopi Butterfly Maiden

12. Bwa Butterfly Mask

13. Mesoamerican Stone Butterflies

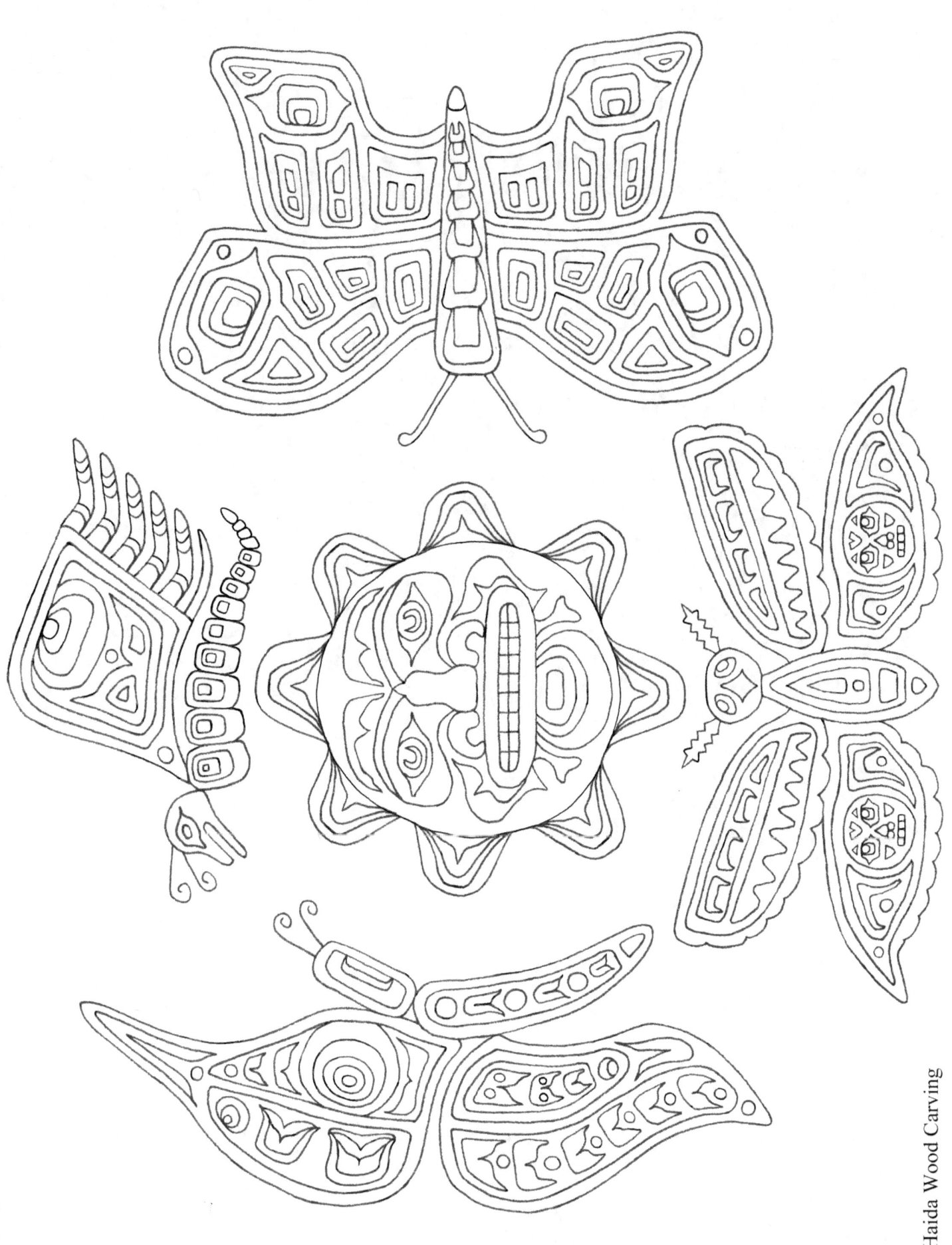

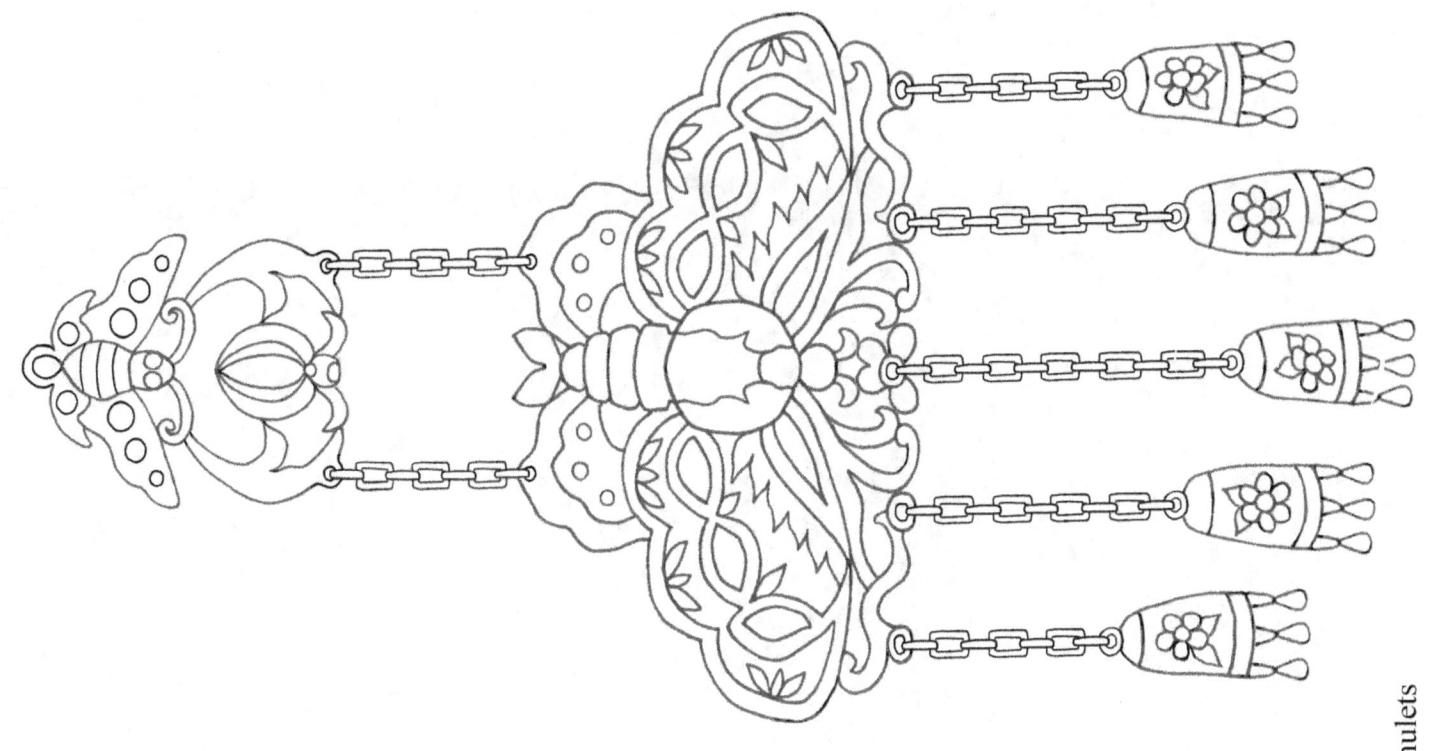

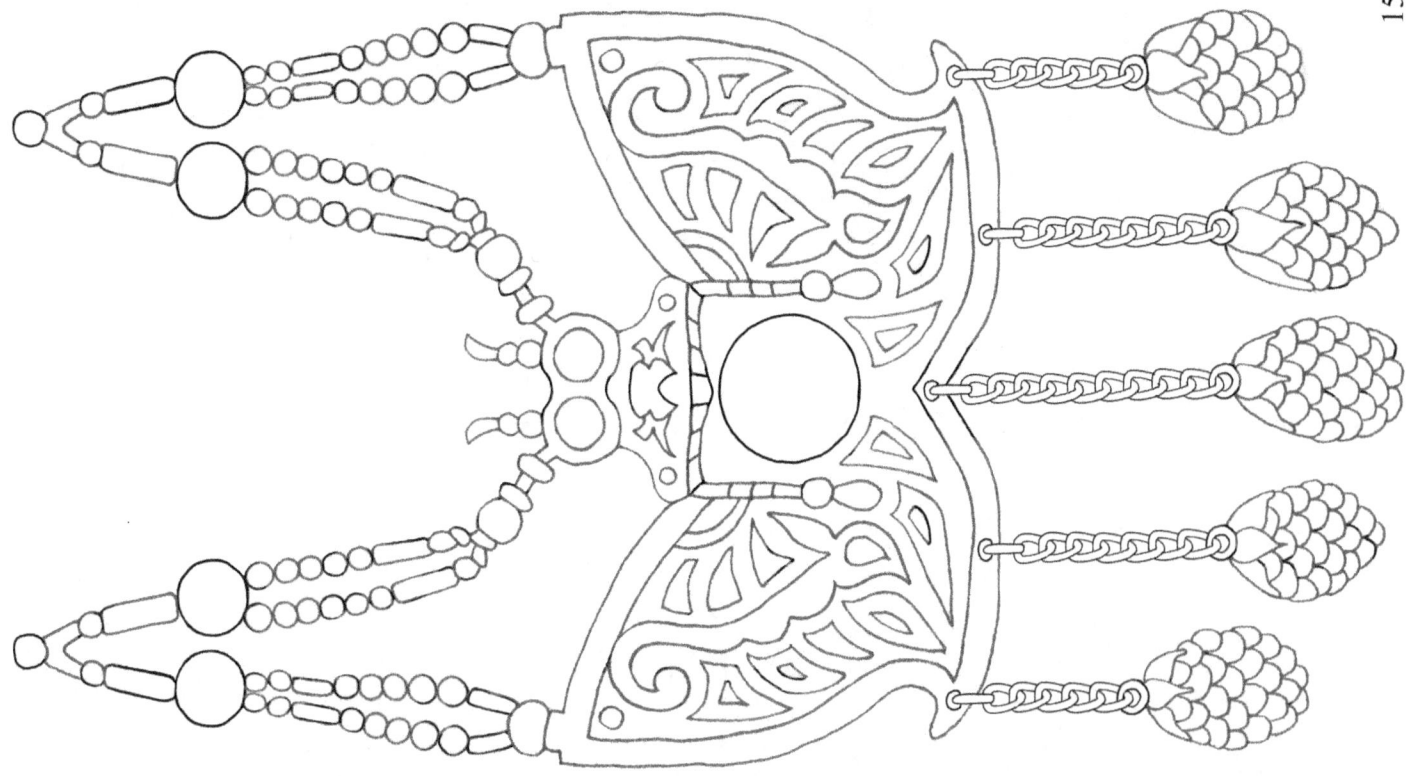

15. Tibetan Silver Amulets

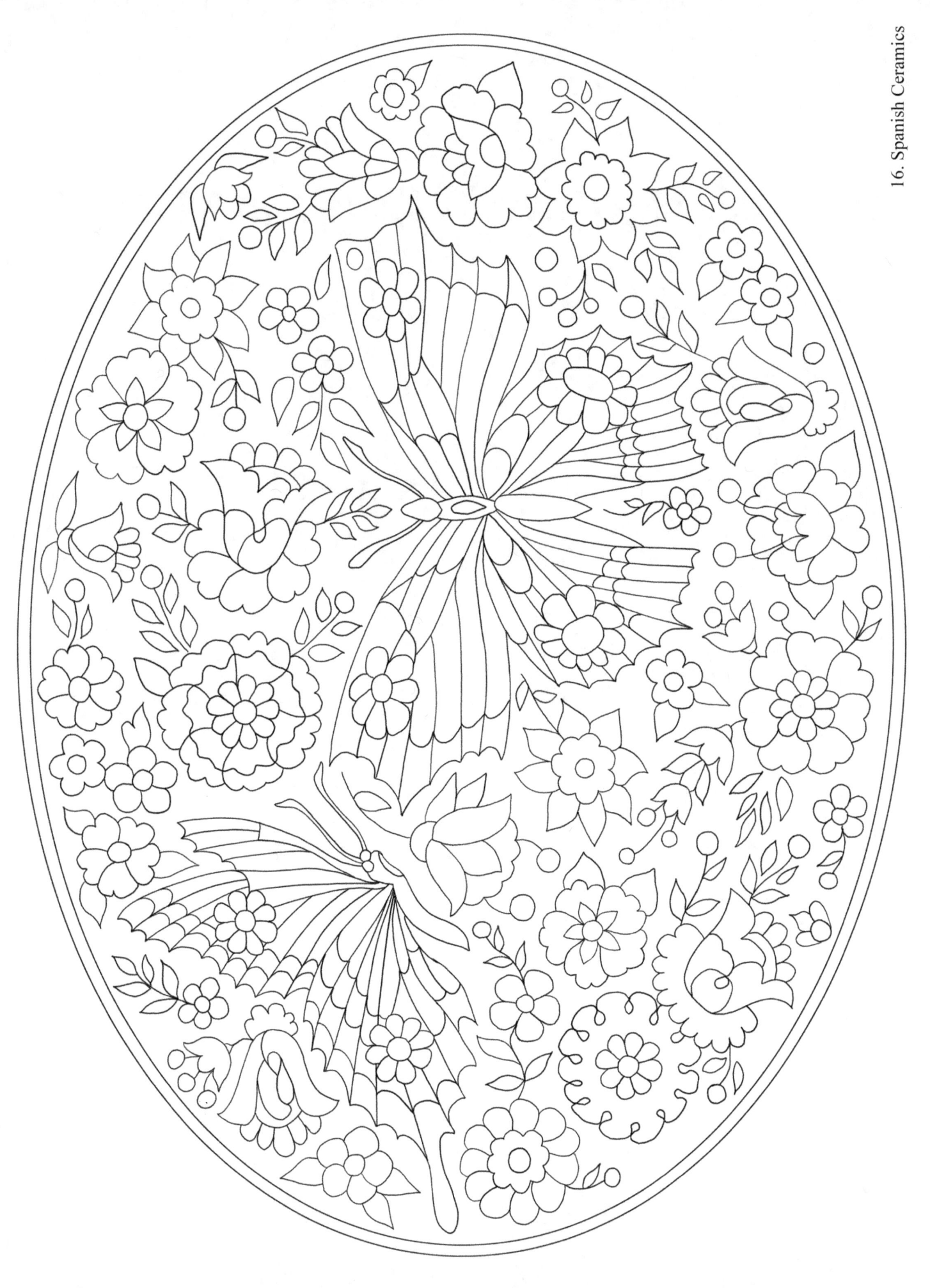

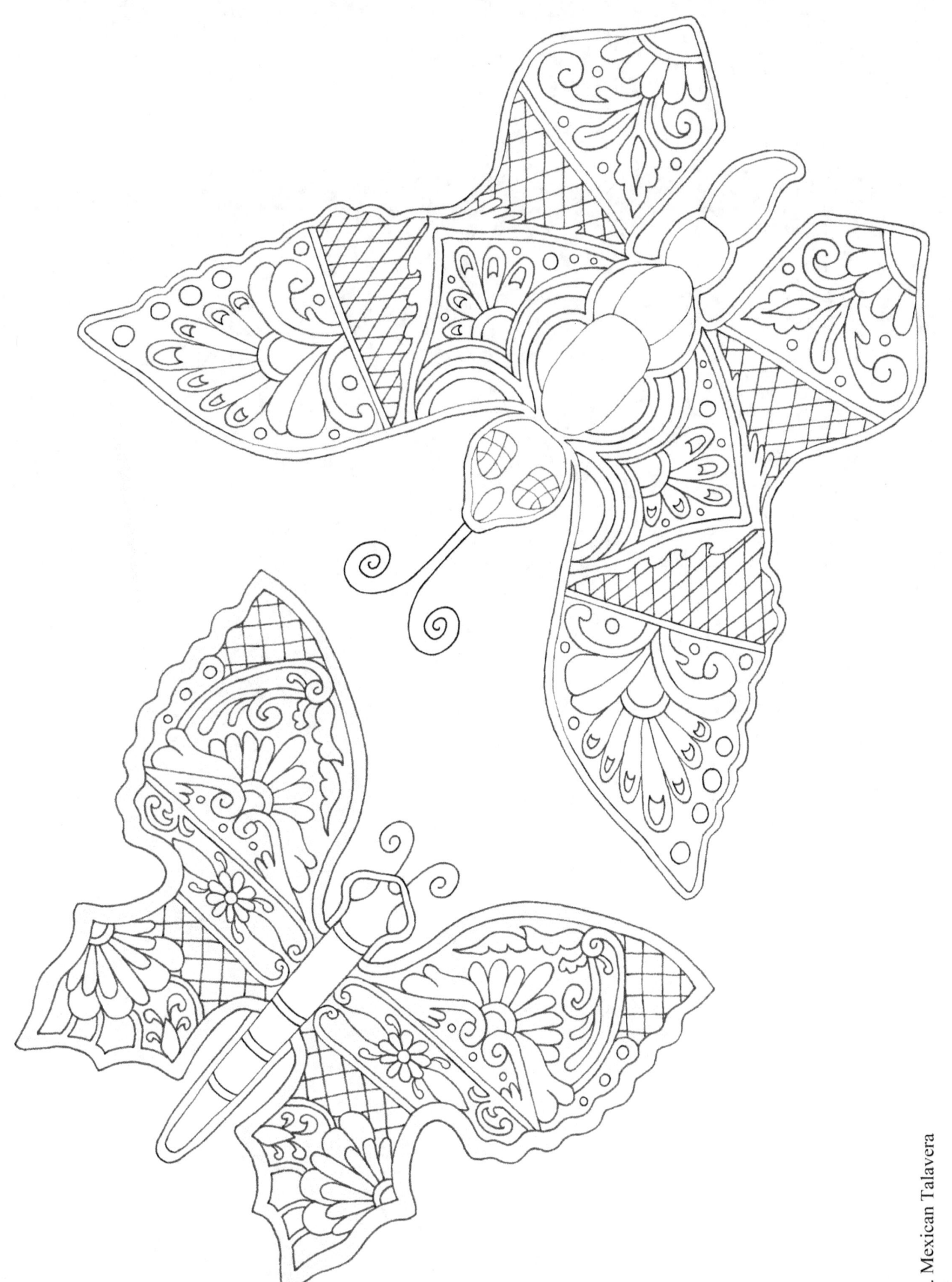

18. Mola Butterfly

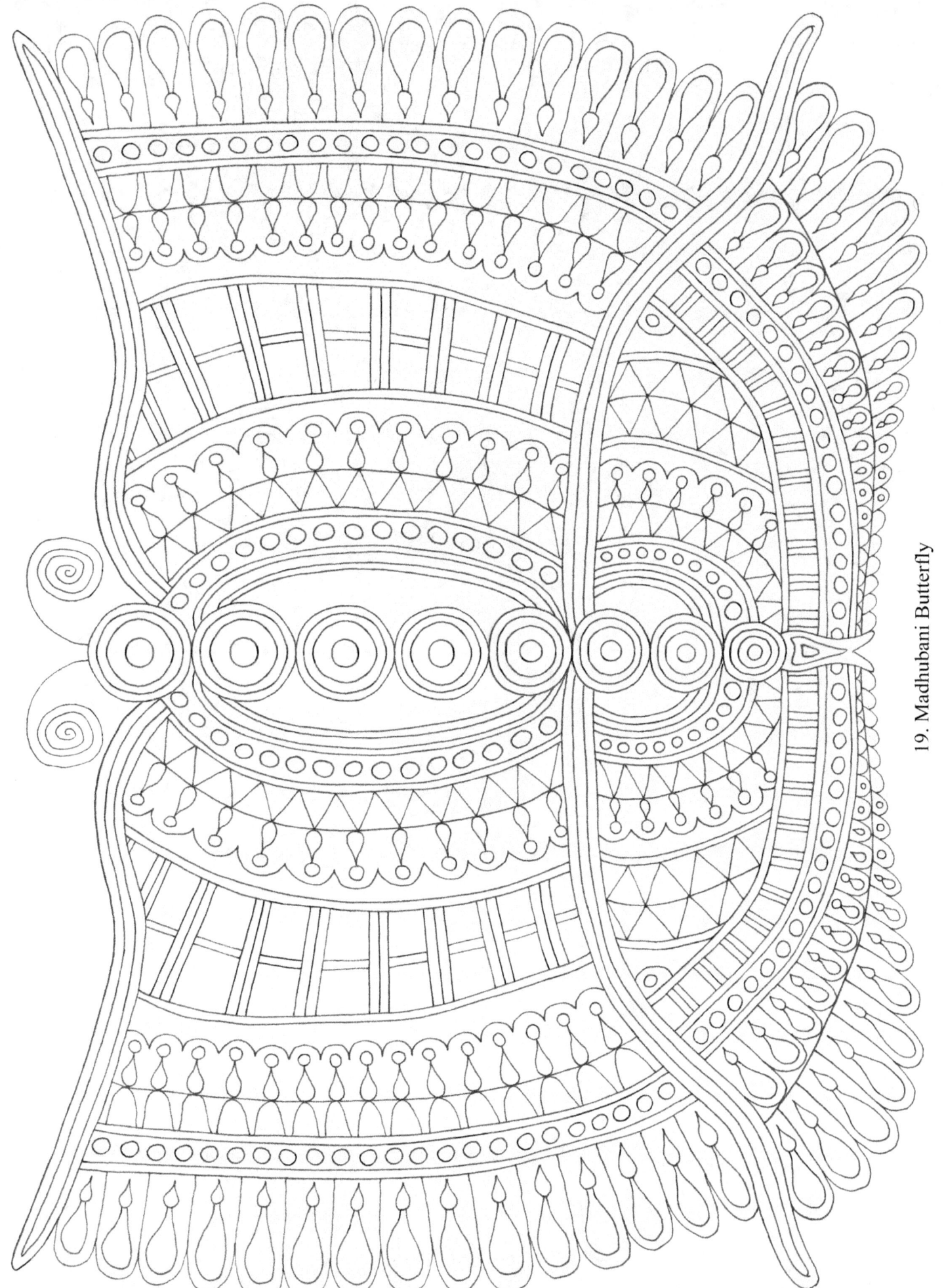

19. Madhubani Butterfly

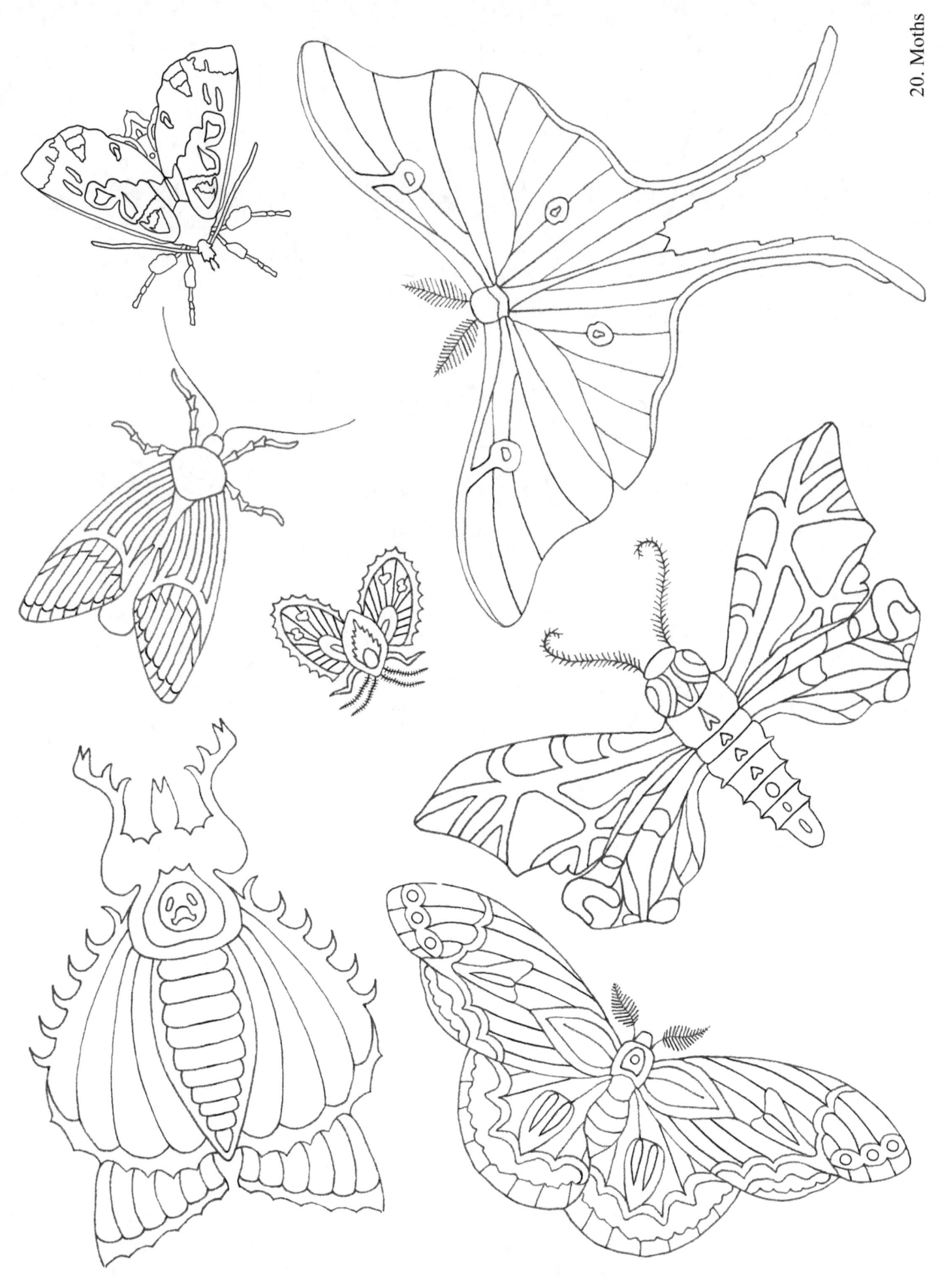

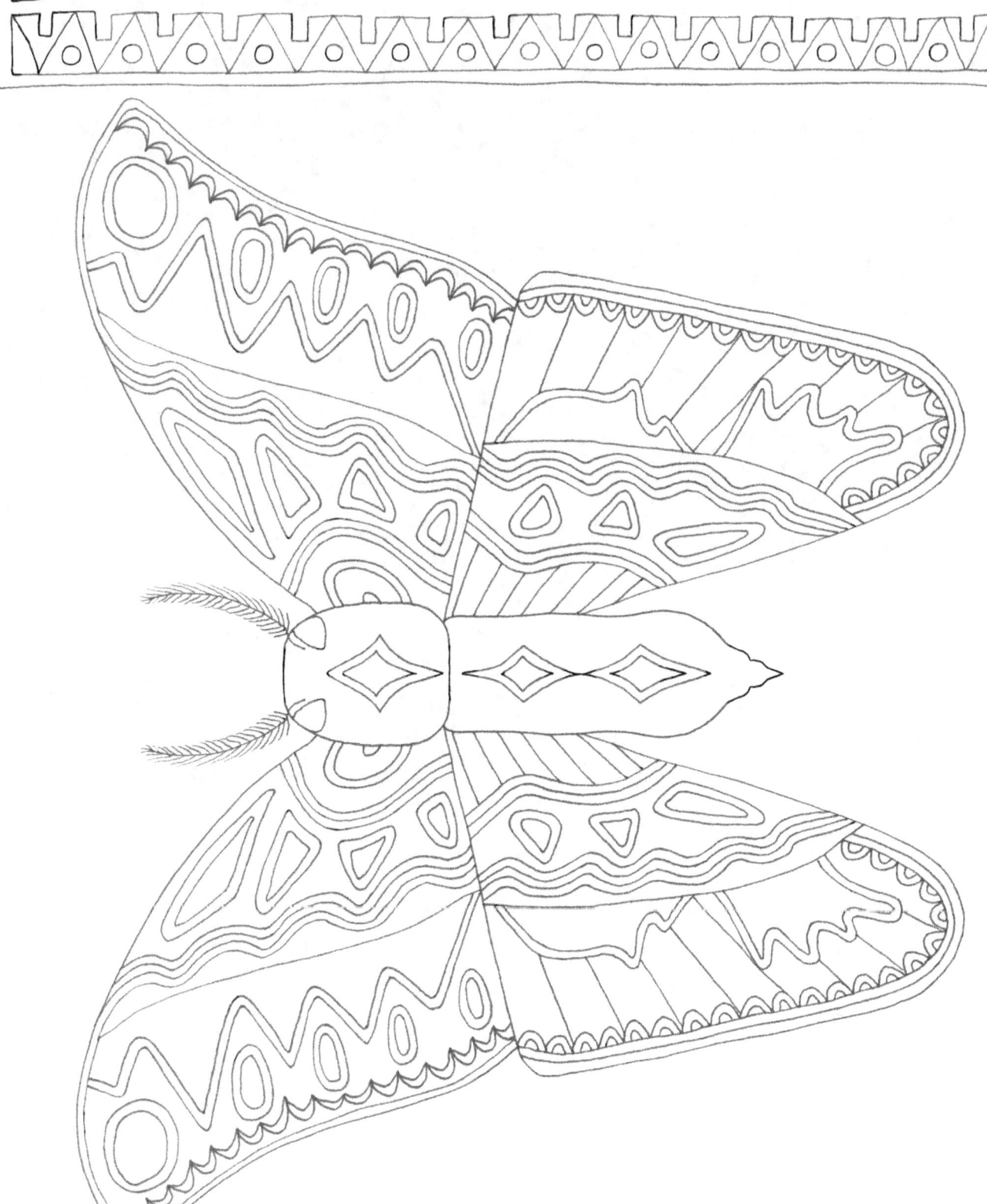

21. Art Deco Moth

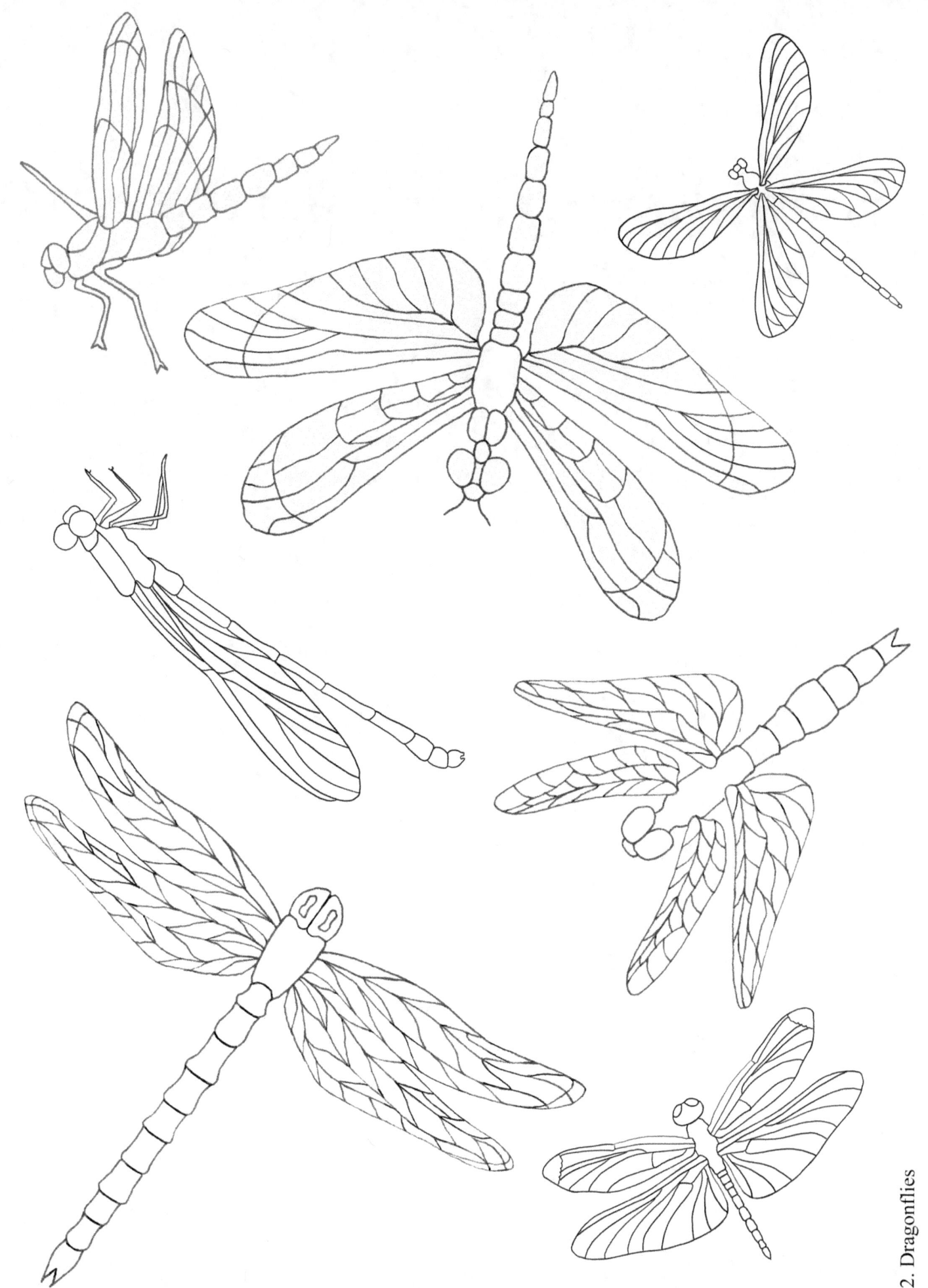

22. Dragonflies

BIZARRE

ART IN

DRAGON

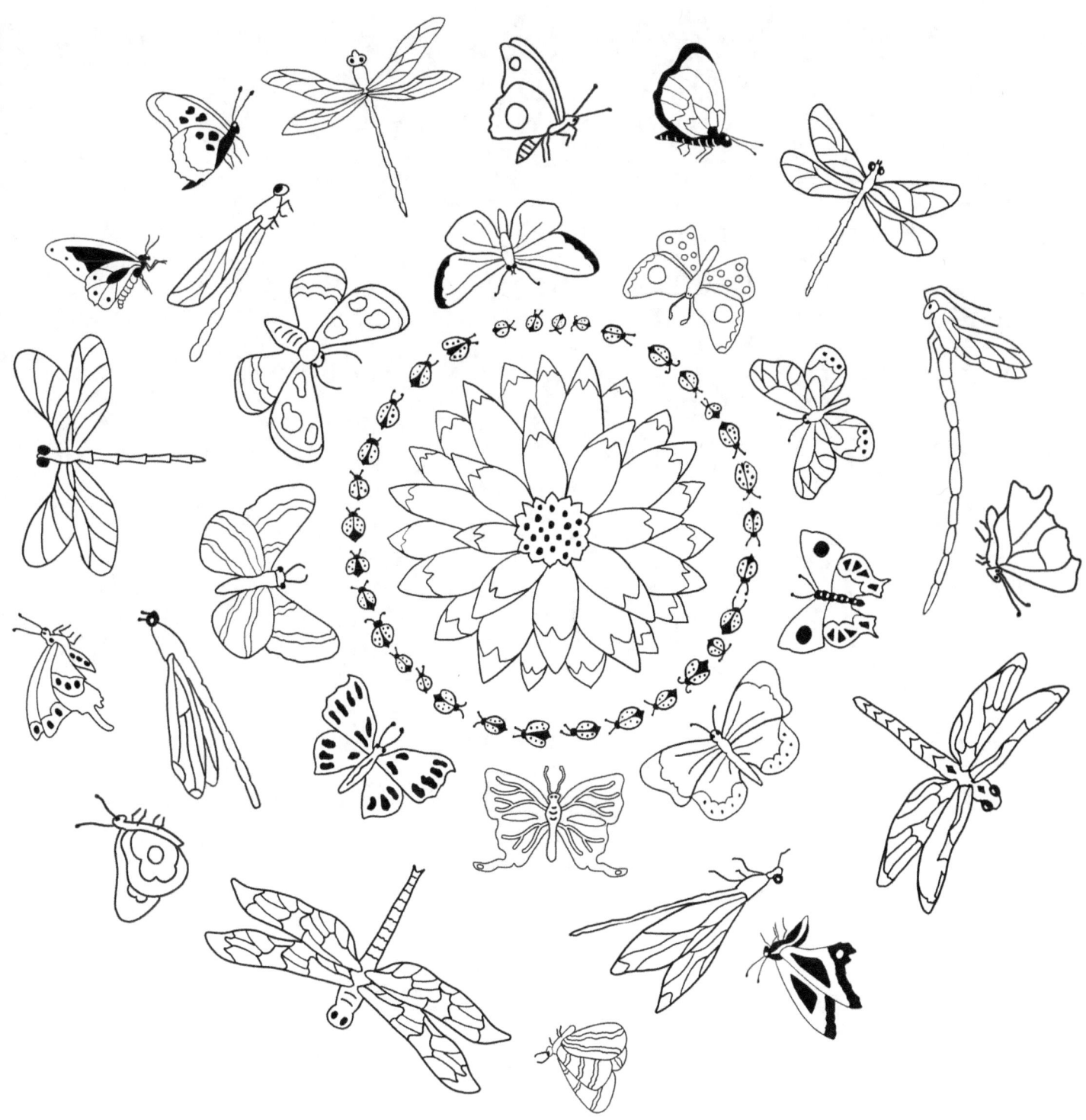

Friendship Butterfly
Created by Akira Yoshizawa ~ Diagramed by Mary Ellen Palmeri

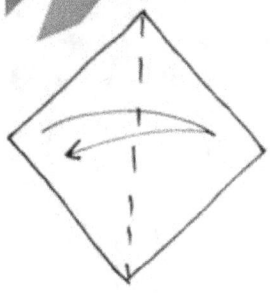

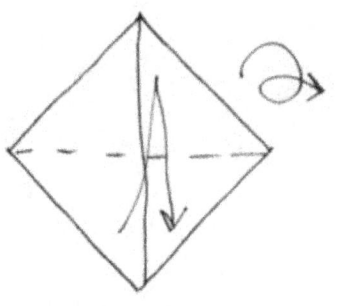

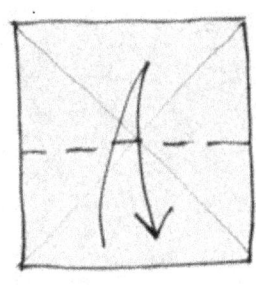

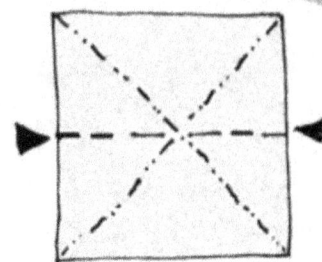

1. With the white side up, fold & unfold diagonal

2. Fold & unfold remaining diagonal, then turn paper over...

3. On this side fold bottom edge up to the top, crease well then unfold again

4. Collapse paper into the shape shown in next step - so this by pushing sides in at the mountain folds & bringing them together to make a triangular form with flaps on each side

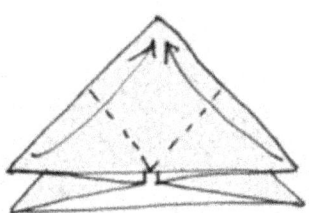

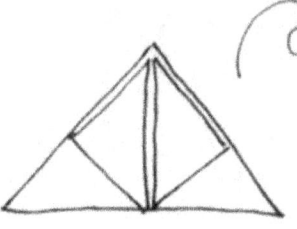

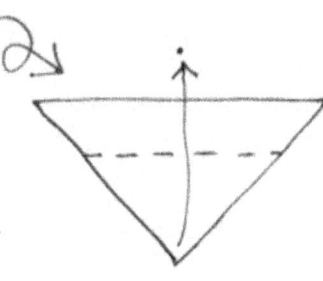

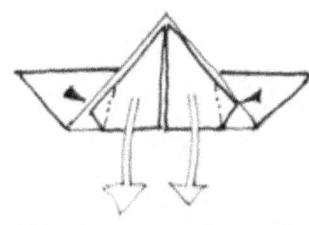

5. Fold top layer of flaps up to meet center top point

6. Turn model over; placing pointed end at the bottom

7. Fold bottom point up above the model (see placement dot)

8. Pull down each flap & at the same time push in & squash the sides edges to look like the next diagram

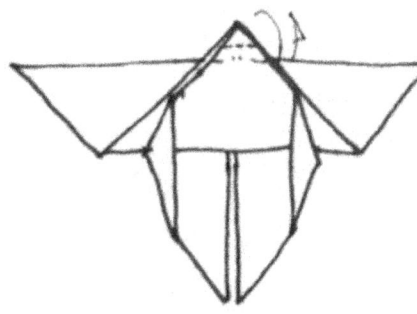

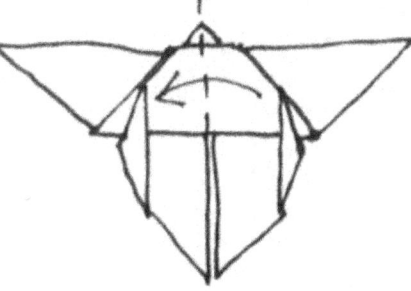

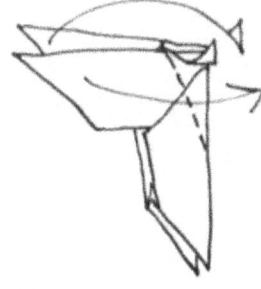

9. Fold top pint behind edge, then fold up just the tip to peek over the edge (see next step)

10. Valley fold model in half

11. Fold top wing over at angle shown; crease goes from behind the head down to end of body (which is hidden under wing), then fold back wing to match

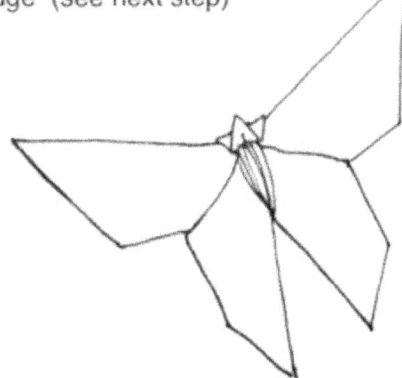

12. Completed Butterfly

The "Friendship Butterfly" was designed by Origami Grandmaster Akira Yoshizawa (1911-2005) to help promote friendship worldwide. His hope was that children of all ages would learn to fold this butterfly and give it away in a friendship gesture - or even better, teach others how to fold it.

tucsonhappenings.com/eZine/0408-august-2016

www.ingramcontent.com/pod-product-compliance
Lightning Source LLC
Chambersburg PA
CBHW08095220526
45467CB00008B/2613